I Made It Back

A Journal About The Horrors of Mental Illness

By Cindy and LaVerne Nyflot

Fairway Press
Lima, Ohio

I MADE IT BACK

FIRST EDITION
Copyright © 1991 by
Cindy and LaVerne Nyflot

All rights reserved. No portion of this book may be reproduced or utilized in any form or by any means, electronic or mechanical including photocopying, without permission in writing from the publisher. Inquiries should be addressed to: Fairway Press, 628 South Main Street, Lima, Ohio 45804.

7760 / ISBN 1-55673-305-4   PRINTED IN U.S.A.

This book is dedicated to Dr. John Jamieson who through his kind understanding, special knowledge of mental illness, and gentle care, brought Cindy back to the world of reality and a life worth living.

TABLE OF CONTENTS

1. My Daughter, Cindy	9
2. Unable to Cope	17
3. Big Plans	21
4. The Diagnosis	25
5. The Trip to New York	27
6. The Minnesota Strip	33
7. Brotherly Love	53
8. A Mother's Perspective	67
9. Locked Up	70
10. A Mother's Perspective	73
11. Freedom	75
12. A Mother's Perspective	81
13. The Institution	89
14. My Escape	105
15. A Mother's Perspective	109
16. Forth Worth, Texas	115
17. A Mother's Perspective	123
18. My Worst Fear	129
19. A Mother's Perspective	133
20. The Cold, Cold Winter	135
21. A Mother's Perspective	141
22. Psychotic	145
23. Picking Up the Broken Pieces	151
24. A Mother's Perspective	157
25. A Mother's Prayer	163
26. Epilogue	165
27. Bipolar Affective Disorder by Dr. John Jamieson	167

PREFACE

In these United States, millions suffer from some form of mental illness: yet so few of the victims have had the courage or the ability to write about their experiences so that others may be helped and know that they are not alone. Sometimes it seems that the general attitude of the public has changed very little since the Dark Ages. However, our attitude certainly changed when our lovely daughter was afflicted with bipolar disorder, better known as manic-depressive illness. We learned our changed attitude the hard way.

Cindy has felt it important to tell her story in the hope that she can help others. Our family feels that if we had been able to find a book like this when she became unwell, it would have given us much needed hope for, at that time, we were learning painfully just how dreadful this illness can be when uncontrolled. The knowledge that most cases can be helped with a simple medication called lithium would have been a great comfort.

Cindy went to Nashville, New York and Fort Worth in a mentally abnormal (hypomanic) state. She ended up on the streets of New York and Fort Worth. Her brothers went to New York with the impossible task of finding their sister who, due to her illness, wanted nothing to do with her family. Incredibly they found her.

Cindy experienced every phase of this dreadful disease, from psychotic symptoms and subsequent severe depression, before getting the help she so desperately needed.

Cindy, who is now stabilized on lithium, tegratol and wellbutrin remembers and tells of her experiences on the streets, on the highways, in the courts, in the state and other hospitals and in doctors' offices.

The stigma associated with this illness is largely due to lack of information. Mental illness is not something that anyone should have to be ashamed of any more than cancer or any other illness. It is so important for people to know that those with mental illness can and do sometimes recover to live normal lives. It is vitally important to know that there is hope.

Cindy and I hope that this journal will help others to recognize the symptoms of this illness. We were so ignorant in the beginning. For example, when Cindy was a teen-ager at high school, she slept and slept. We had no idea of what was wrong and apparently the doctors we consulted also had no idea that this might be a symptom of mental illness.

Helping the public to better understand bipolar disorder so that it will be easier for them to reach out in warmth and compassion to those afflicted is the most important goal of this journal.

Chapter 1

MY DAUGHTER, CINDY

(LaVerne) Saturday, June 2, 1983

It was 6:30 p.m. when I returned home from a nearby town where our center for mentally handicapped adults had participated in a parade. It had been a gray, gloomy day with a cold wind and rain putting a damper on the festivities. I walked into the house, thankful to be home and longing to fall into an easy chair after the exhausting day, but as I entered, my son, Jeff, met me at the door. He tried to be as tactful as possible, but nothing could soften the blow of his words.

"Cindy is in New York City!" he said. "She'll be calling back at seven to talk to you. Dad talked to her for half an hour trying to persuade her to come home, but she says she is not coming home!"

The news took my breath away. "New York? Oh God! New York!" She had told us that she was going to the lake with a friend during the quarter break. "Oh, God, what are we going to do?" Oscar and Jeff were now on each side ushering me to a chair by the kitchen table, expecting that I would feel faint, but there was no time for that. Cindy would be calling back soon and I had to be calm and in control. I simply had to persuade her to come back home.

About three weeks prior to this, Cindy had been diagnosed as having bipolar disorder, better know as manic-depressive illness. When the doctor told her this, she refused to accept the diagnosis. It is very common for patients with this disorder to refuse to believe they are ill. He prescribed lithium which is a natural and simple salt substance often found in mountain stream beds and which is a successful treatment in a large percentage of cases.

When I called the doctor to learn more about the severity of her illness, I got the impression that her condition was not severe. He pointed out that she was not awake seven nights in a row or anything like that, and he assured me that her high and low moods were within normal limits. I relaxed a little, but nevertheless pleaded with Cindy to take the lithium.

AND NOW SHE WAS IN NEW YORK! Oscar, Jeff and I were stunned. We sat in deathlike silence, waiting for the phone to ring. The only sounds that could be heard were the splattering of rain on the window and the clanging of metal as Jeff doggedly kept working on our dishwasher which had been on the blink. It was an unforgettable time of torture. It was not the first, nor yet the last!

I dredged up memories of happier times. The happiest times of my life were the days my children were born. Cindy was our New Year's Day baby. We already had two sons whom we dearly loved, and I was resigned to having a third son; but I wanted a girl so badly and on January 1, 1963, I heard the doctor say, "It's a nice baby girl!" I can still remember the feeling of joy, contentment and gratefulness welling up and overflowing. She had black hair, black eyes and olive skin. How did I get this darling, Oriental baby? Foggily, I began thanking the doctor for my girl, as if he had something to do with it, and I kept up my giddy prattle until the doctor cleared his throat and with just a hint of gruffness and impatience in his tone said, "Yes, yes, you have your girl now." I heard the nurse chuckle. That cleared my head and shut me up for the time being.

As a little girl she was athletic and energetic. She loved to show off by standing on her head. Her brothers made a little tomboy of her, swinging her by the feet, and challenging her to do whatever they did. And she loved it.

Then one winter's evening when she was about nine years old, I came home from choir practice to find Cindy in a daze. Her little friend told me that she had been standing on the sled when someone jerked the sled to get it going, and she fell, hitting her head on the ice. I became concerned when she kept asking when we had gotten our new couch. She seemed to have lost her memory. I immediately called the doctor, but he didn't seem to think that she needed to be hospitalized. I put her to bed, but she began throwing up and was feverish. I called the doctor again, but he didn't think we should bring her to the hospital. By morning she had stopped throwing up, but she had such a terrible headache. I kept putting cold cloths on her forehead until she finally went to sleep. After a couple of days she seemed fine again, except for one thing — she could no longer stand on her head, nor could she tolerate being upside-down from that day until this.

Late one evening, about a year after the head injury, Jeff was watching television after everyone had gone to bed. He heard a loud thud and other strange noises and went upstairs to check. When he turned the light on in Cindy's room, he found her on the floor under the bed, arms and legs flailing about. He yelled in panic, "Something's wrong with Cindy!" Oscar and I came running to find Cindy having a grand mal seizure. We didn't know what a seizure was at that time. I tried to hold her, but she kept fighting. Oscar grabbed her and ran with her to the car. We raced to the hospital 13 miles away. By the time the doctor got to the hospital she was beginning to come out of the seizure. The doctor made an appointment for her in Fargo, and Dilantin (generic name, phenytoin) was prescribed. After a year without seizures, the Dilantin was discontinued and there have been no more seizures.

During the next few years, before reaching high school, Cindy didn't seem the worse for the wear; but then the struggle with bipolar disorder began although, at the time, we had no idea what was happening. In her sophomore year in high school she had come down with infectious mononucleosis and hepatitis (liver trouble). After that she never got over being tired, at least not in the winter months. I could hardly get her up for school except on those days when she was to play the piano for the chorus. Even then it was a battle, but she would finally drag herself out of bed. She slept 16 to 18 hours each day. She was consistently late. When her classmates were asked to predict what each classmate would be doing in the future, they predicted that Cindy would someday arrive late for her own concert in Carnegie Hall.

We took her to doctors, but they attributed her tiredness to the mononucleosis, her age, and other things. Later, when she was a junior in high school, she also lost her appetite and at that point we decided to take her to the Mayo Clinic. The diagnosis there was, "She's fine. Kids like to sleep." Later still, in the spring, she had Vitamin B12 shots which, of course, did not help.

Although generally better during her senior high school year, Cindy continued to sleep excessively. In the fall of that year there were special meetings at our church and afterward some young people met at our home for informal Bible studies. During that time Cindy committed her life to God. I was not fully aware of the extent of her commitment until she told me that she had been upset by a textbook that was being used in the home economics class. She was convinced that the textbook was promulgating values which were not compatible with the Christian faith. The emphasis was on doing your own thing, using values clarification to determine your individual lifestyle. Every lifestyle, except the traditional, seemed to be acceptable. Cindy expressed her concerns at school and had a rough time from classmates and teachers because of her stand. Nevertheless, she seemed to cope well with the adversity.

During her first year in college she was not only tired but also depressed. Up to this point we did not realize that just being chronically tired could be a sign of depression. We attributed her depression to our having unexpectedly lost our largest supply of cream for our creamery business. This loss meant the loss of the business itself, and the doors of the creamery were closed just before Christmas, 1981. This devastating blow left the whole family in a state of insecurity and helplessness.

The two boys had worked with their dad, one managing the convenience store and the other working at the creamery and ice business. All bills came due at once, so in order to pay, it was necessary to sell the equipment for a fraction of what it was worth. After another year, it became evident that it would be necessary to sell the convenience store and the ice business to get all the bills paid. They had to be sold at a tremendous loss, but bankruptcy was something we wanted to avoid at all costs. Over a period of three years, Oscar and the boys had been fighting this financial battle, and it took a toll on our family.

Unwittingly, we blamed Cindy's depression on this because, by this time, other members of the family were also depressed. One son entered a treatment center for alcoholism.

I learned that "breaking out in a cold sweat" was not just an expression, but a reality. Each night for months, Oscar would go to bed with the covers piled high on top of him only to freeze until the bed shook. In the mornings he and the blanket next to him would be sopping wet. This went on for about two years, and it seemed no wonder that he eventually succumbed to depression. It would not have been so hard if he had not had his boys in the business with him. Now they were floundering without a means of making a living as there just were no jobs available at this time.

During the summers through high school and college, Cindy worked at our convenience store which was located in a town 50 miles from our home, so we were not fully aware of how she felt in the summers. She didn't want to come home much in the summer, and we didn't understand this at the time. We had no idea that she had a tendency to become "high" (hypomanic) in the summertime. She was a terrific worker and sometimes would work all night cleaning the store. Nor did we know that she was sleeping very little at night. Her brother complained about her irritability, her choice of friends, her boisterous talk (especially about her planned trip to Nashville), her compulsive need to have her apartment and the store spotlessly clean and her angry flare-ups over trivialities. This was not like our Cindy at all. These were symptoms of her illness, but we did not know that and proceeded to comfort ourselves with facile explanations for her behavior. Needless to say, the possibility of mental illness was never considered. The death, from an overdose, of a classmate friend and the departure of her boyfriend from the town made our rationalizations seem all the more plausible. To us it seemed clear that insecurity and indecision about the future must have caused her personality change.

During the summer of 1982, after college, she came to a decision to go in the fall to Nashville, Tennessee, to find work. How and why she made this decision was never clear. There appeared to be no rhyme or reason for it — she just made up her mind to go to Nashville, and that is what she eventually did. She saved every check and by Thursday, September 16, 1982, she had accumulated $1,500 and, as we later learned, she left for Nashville at 3:00 a.m. that day. That same night her brother was taken to the hospital. I could take in stride losing the businesses, but about this time, I felt I was living in a nightmare. Things couldn't get worse, I thought. But I was wrong for things did just keep getting worse! I had kept trying to encourage my family by insisting that there is a reason for what goes on in our lives and that God would see us through it all. I felt a need to be strong for my family's sake. It would have been easy to allow myself to fall to pieces and hope that someone would pick me up and put me back together again, but instead I clung tenaciously to my faith and trust in God and the promises of His Word, and I was given the strength needed for the day, making it possible to carry on one day at a time and to come through it all in one piece.

Cindy went to Nashville by way of Myrtle Beach, South Carolina. By the time she got to Knoxville, Tennessee, where she had intended to take in the World's Fair, it was clear that she was getting depressed again. She didn't have the energy to go to the Fair, so she went on to Nashville. Every day we got tearful calls from her. She said that she was too tired and depressed to look for work. Each time I'd plead, "Cindy, you don't have to stay in Nashville, please come home." After two weeks of that she did start for home on October 5, 1982.

She had thought that when she came home she could work at the store again, but on November 7, 1982, the doors of our store were closed. Cindy cried most of the time. It was another monumental disappointment for her. Any suggestion that she should go to a doctor or psychiatrist fell on deaf ears. At my suggestion she went to the Twin Cities to stay with her cousin and look for work. I thought she needed to be with young, happy people; but, of course, that didn't help at all. She left for Minneapolis on Monday, November 8, but returned home the next day. I didn't know that her problem was a chemical imbalance and that no amount of socializing would help. When she came home, she reluctantly went to a local doctor who prescribed an antidepressant which didn't help.

On January 10, she went back to the Twin Cities as a friend talked to her son at H & R Block, and he said there would be a job for Cindy if she came down. However, one week was as long as she could tolerate it. When she called begging to come home, we tried to encourage her to stay and give herself a little more time, but she was so desperate that she threatened to commit suicide.

We got in our car and raced to Minneapolis to bring her home. We forced her to go to a psychiatrist then. Now, five months later she was in New York! Sick and alone!

R . . .I . . . N . . . G! We all jumped at the harsh sound! I grabbed the phone.

"Hello. Cindy?"

"Hi, Mom!"

"Cindy, are you really in New York?"

"Yes, and I'm having a great time. It's so exciting here!"

"Aren't you coming back to finish your course at business college?"

"Oh, I might come back in the fall to finish. I love it here, and I'm going to get a job. Tomorrow I'm going to be selling ice cream in front of Macy's. You know, those big push carts!"

"Cindy, your doctor says you have bipolar disorder, and that you need lithium!"

"I'M FINE. CAN'T YOU UNDERSTAND THAT?"

"Cindy, may I read some of your symptoms of bipolar disorder? I had Carla look up some information on it."

"I suppose."

"I'll read the symptoms: 'Pressure of speech, motor hyperactivity, reduced need for sleep, flight of ideas, grandiosity or poor judgment, aggressiveness and possibly hostility." There was silence at the other end, then:

"Yeah, I can make an appointment with a doctor, I suppose, just to please you."

"Cindy, won't you please come home?"

"NOT YET, AND IF MY BROTHERS COME LOOKING FOR ME, I'LL DISAPPERAR, AND YOU'LL NEVER SEE ME AGAIN!"

"Will you call tomorrow?"

"Sure. Just think, I'll be here on the 4th of July. Is that ever going to be fun!"

"Where are you sleeping? Do you have any money left?"

"I've been sleeping in my car because I got my money stolen the first day I came here!"

"Where is your car?"

"It's parked at 42nd and 8th in a parking lot."

"Do you still have your kitty?"

"OF COURSE! I take her out for walks."

"Cindy, I love you. Will you call us tomorrow morning?"

"Mom, you sound brokenhearted. I'm going to be fine. 'BYE!"

The next days, weeks and months were a blur of grief, anxiety, heartache and exhaustion interspersed with panic. However, there was also at times an inexplicable peace — "a peace that passes understanding."

Chapter 2

UNABLE TO COPE

(Cindy) January 18, 1983

I had been in Minneapolis for eight days, working at H & R Block. Each morning I would wake up with a sensation of a heavy and persistent weight on my chest, and I found it almost impossible to get up. Living with two roommates was frustrating. Although I showered at least once daily, I felt grungy and dirty. The 45 minute drive through traffic to get to work was nerve-racking and I felt incompetent on the job. I was totally miserable and had a desperate longing for the comfort and safety of home.

One evening I decided I could stand it no longer and called home. By the time Mom answered the telephone, I was hysterical. The misery and hopelessness I felt came pouring out in tears and sobs. "Mom I have to come home. I can't stand it here any longer," I sobbed.

I was terrified that she would want me to stay longer and that was exactly what she asked me to do.

"Cindy, won't you please try to stay just a few more days? You haven't given yourself time to adjust," she pleaded.

I interrupted her, screaming, "IF I CAN'T COME HOME, I WILL KILL MYSELF!" And I meant it. I had never verbalized this feeling previously, though I often thought it was the only solution to my miserable life. My words had an immediate impact on my Mom's attitude. In a quiet, but firm voice she cautioned, "Cindy, stay right where you are. Dad and I will be down there right away. It will take about six hours, so we will be there about midnight. Will you stay right where you are, Cindy? We don't want you driving tonight!"

"Yes, Mom, but please hurry!" I sobbed.

I was so relieved that I fell back on the couch exhausted and slept the best I had slept since leaving home.

When my parents arrived at midnight, I was calm. I was feeling better having them with me; but when they again started trying to persuade me to keep working, the same paralyzing, awful feeling came over me. They quit nagging when they realized I would not be persuaded. We stayed in a motel that night.

January 19, 1983

When morning came, I refused to go back to work. Mom then started making telephone calls. When I realized what she was doing, I told her firmly that going to a psychiatrist was out of the question. I was NOT, NOT mentally ill! However, I did agree to see a counselor and that afternoon my parents took me to her office.

The counselor was very nice, but at that time, none of us knew that no amount of talking, no amount of friends, no amount of new clothes or fun activity could help me. What I needed, we all learned much later, was for my illness to be diagnosed and treated!

All I wanted was to go home to sleep and be left alone. My parents finally agreed that I could come home on one condition — THAT I SEE A PSYCHIATRIST! It was very hard for me to agree to that, but I wanted to go home so badly that I agreed to their terms.

January 20, 1983

We filled the two cars with my belongings and started for home. Dad drove one car and Mom, the other. I was so relieved to be going home that I fell asleep and slept all the way.

January 21, 1983

The next afternoon Mom woke me up with the words, "I've made an appointment with a psychiatrist for Monday, January 24th!" "You didn't waste any time, did you!" I growled. Of one thing I was sure — I did not need a psychiatrist. I would go simply because that was the agreement.

January 24, 1983

The day of the appointment came much too quickly. To avoid going, I used every kind of dodge, from burying my head in my pillow and telling Mom that I was sick, to blatantly yelling, "I WON'T GO! I don't need a psychiatrist, YOU DO!"

But I lost the battle.

That afternoon when we got to the psychiatrist's office, I told Mom, "I hope he's short, fat and bald!" Just then a young, handsome man walked by, and I whispered to Mom. "I sure hope that isn't the psychiatrist! Do you think he is?" Without thinking Mom said, "I suppose he is." That did it! I jumped up and stated, "I'm not going to HIM, I'm LEAVING!" Mom wisely changed her tune by saying that it probably wasn't this man, and that I should wait and see. I sat down again, but I was extremely restless and agitated.

Finally, we were told to come in, and SURE ENOUGH, it was that same man that had walked by us. I shot Mom an angry, reproachful look, but she avoided eye contact with me. She was well aware of what I was thinking and was worried as to what I might do.

She started by telling him about how I would sleep excessively in the winters and then change completely in the summers, becoming full of energy, talkative, enthusiastic and ambitious. I, myself, had long been aware of a marked dislike for winter and a great love of summer. I was convinced that the seasons caused the changes in my personality and I planned to go to a warmer climate as soon as possible. THAT, I was sure, would solve my problem. As for this psychiatrist,

I simply clammed up! I would not discuss anything whatever with him.

The psychiatrist and Mom discussed me for about half an hour; and, in spite of all the emphasis my Mom made of the changes in my personality, the doctor just couldn't diagnose what was causing it. He thought that I was depressed. The winter/summer thing was a conundrum to him.

I went home more angry than ever but took comfort from the fact that nothing had been said about mental illness. Anyway, I knew I was not mentally ill, so why should I ever have to go back to that psychiatrist? He prescribed some antidepressant which, as I expected, didn't help. Why couldn't everyone, especially my parents, leave me alone? All I wanted to do was sleep.

March, 1983

I had made it through one year of college, and Mom kept suggesting that I should go back to school. I still didn't care about anything. I felt numb and lethargic with no interest in the future, or the present for that matter. Finally, they insisted that I enroll in a vocational school, but there were no openings. Undaunted, they took me to a business college in Fargo where I enrolled in a legal secretarial course which was to begin on Monday, April 4, 1983.

Chapter 3

BIG PLANS!

(Cindy) April 4, 1983

By the time I entered business college, I was beginning to feel somewhat better. I saw the psychiatrist twice in February but did not keep any further appointments and discontinued his medication.

I rented an efficiency apartment and furnished it. I was told it was cozy, but I was not well enough to feel much of anything. I simply had no capacity to take pleasure in my apartment or anything else. I was doing what I was doing because my parents wanted it so. Moreover, I wasn't so sick that I didn't realize that I had to do something with my life.

When my parents left me alone in Fargo, I felt totally abandoned by everyone. I had no friends in Fargo, and I didn't have the ambition or the desire to find any. Each day I went to school in the morning and slept in the afternoon. About the only conversation I had each day was by telephone with one of my parents or brothers. During the first quarter, in spite of my depression, I found the classes very easy. My grades were excellent, but I didn't learn this until much later.

May 27, 1983

I became acquainted with one of the girls at school, and we made plans to attend a show together about two weeks before the spring break.

As I was getting ready to go to the show, I suddenly felt so exceptionally happy and good about myself. Everything seemed wonderful — even glorious. I decided that my happiness was due to my having found a friend at last. I felt exhilarated! It was as if I had become a new person! Just then the telephone rang and, for a change, I grabbed it eagerly. As usual, it was Mom. "Mom, I feel just wonderful tonight — almost too good!" I exclaimed. "Kelly and I are going to a show. I've never felt quite like this before — euphoric." I became angry when, instead of being pleased that I felt so good, she immediately expressed concern. I therefore hastily ended the conversation and continued to get ready for the show as I was supremely confident that my newfound happiness was due to my having a friend.

Kelly and I hit it off really well. When I learned that she had relatives in New York City, I suggested that we go there for spring break. She agreed that it was a good idea, but didn't seem very enthusiastic. However, she assured me that she would go along. That settled it. We planned that in about a week we'd be heading for New York City!

There were so many things to do before we were to leave, not the least of which was to go home to get my rent money and as much additional spending money as possible. I had some unemplyment money saved, but I wouldn't get far on that. I had no intention of telling my folks that I was planning to go to New York. Even though my thinking was clouded and becoming more so every day, I had enough sense not to tell them. Instead I told them I was going to Detroit Lakes, Minnesota, with Kelly. They were so happy for me.

My parents believed me. Until now I hadn't given them any reason not to trust me. I had given my life over to God when I was a senior, and since then my desire had been to live a life pleasing to Him.

They had no idea what the symptoms of mental illness were, and neither did I. I was to learn what it all meant later, much later. Being secretive and telling lies, often elaborate lies, is common among those suffering from the hypomanic phase of this illness. However, these symptoms were the least of all the hideous effects it was to have on my life.

I wasn't sleeping much any more, but I didn't know that insomnia was also a sign of hypomania. I thought it was just due to the excitement of going to New York.

Chapter 4

THE DIÁGNOSIS

(Cindy) June 21, 1983

Before leaving for New York, I had to do one more thing. I just had to go to see my psychiatrist to show him how well I was. No more depression for me! How silly of my folks to have forced me to see this psychiatrist!

I marched into his office with an "I'll show him!" attitude. Again, in my ignorance I did not know that grandiosity and impairment of judgment were signs of hypomania. He took one look at me and made the correct diagnosis. He said in no uncertain terms, "Cindy, you have bipolar disorder. We have lithium which works well in about 80 percent of cases. You should start taking lithium right away before your condition worsens. Right now I believe you are within normal limits." I couldn't understand what he was talking about. Couldn't he see that I was not sick? What an idiot! I certainly would never take any pills. The truth of the matter was that I was much more sick than he realized because his words meant absolutely nothing to me at this point. I shrugged off everything he said and walked out of his office like a zombie. He didn't try to stop me, or try to persuade or force me to take the pills. I just left. No muss, no fuss. It was to be the beginning of my trip to hell and the doctor, who knew about this illness and its devastating effects, just let me walk out without a word of warning except to say, "If you change your mind about taking lithium, give me a call."

After rushing back to the apartment, I called home to tell my folks that the stupid psychiatrist had said that I had a biploar disorder, whatever that meant. I told them that he was dead wrong and that I had never felt so good! Mom sounded very worried and begged me to take the pills as they wouldn't hurt and might help. I didn't see any need of that at all, and told her so!

During the next three days I busied myself getting ready to take off with Kelly to New York. On top of all the other preparations, I had to arrange a sitter for my kitty until we came back. The grandiosity was still with me for I made reservations at the *Waldorf Astoria*, no less!

The sleeplessness continued, but it didn't concern me as I was sure that I knew the cause. I was getting very irritable, and my usual social inhibitions were beginning to fade. Now I wanted friends again, and I jabbered nonstop. Insomnia, irritability, increased energy level, impaired judgment, excessive people-seeking behavior, excessive talkativeness (hyperloquacity) and grandiosity — I had all the hypomanic signs and symptoms, but had not the faintest idea that I was ill!

Chapter 5

THE TRIP TO NEW YORK

(Cindy) June 24, 1983

Friday, June 24th, the beginning of the spring break, arrived before I knew it. I had so much fun anticipating the trip to New York that I just knew the trip itself would be a blast. I hurried over to Kelly's home. "New York, here we come!!" I cheered. Her reaction was not at all what I had expected or wanted to hear. "Oh, Cindy, I can't come along. My boyfriend won't let me!" she complained. I wonder why? It was just an innocent little 1,600 mile trip to one of the biggest cities in the world. She pretended that she was disappointed, but she really wasn't. I was desperately disappointed right away, but in my manic mood nothing could discourage me for long. "I'm going anyway. Nothing is going to stop me!" I retorted. She responded with, "I thought you'd say that," and with that we parted, but I remained as determined as ever.

Since Kelly wasn't going with me, I decided to take my kitty along. I had been to New York with my parents on two previous occasions, but I had never stayed at the Waldorf Astoria! As I could no longer reason things out, it had not occurred to me that I would not be able to afford to stay in such an expensive hotel. I had collected around $375 for the trip. How long would that last? I was not dumb, just sick and getting more sick each day. The aggravating effect of the excitement and activity was catapulting me into a higher and giddier state of mania. I had no idea that I was losing my judgment and could not make rational decisions. I was now extremely hyperactive and restless though still euphoric in an odd sort of way. As if all that was not enough, I was beginning to feel a diabolical attraction to the dregs of humanity and a corresponding hatred for the rich and powerful. It started with hating the psychiatrist for saying that I was sick, and it kept escalating to include everyone who looked prosperous, authoritative or just plain decent. Just what I needed when going to New York City!

I looked at the down-and-out as poor wayward souls, victims of an uncaring society. I would be their angel of light who would help them out of their terrible situation — my first delusion! I hadn't figured out how yet, but cigarette smoking was another disgusting, but comparatively harmless offshoot of this illness, so I would give cigarettes to anyone who asked or even looked as though he would like one. Some help that was!!

Things were getting more ridiculous by the hour. After I left Kelly and got back to my apartment, I decided that if I was going to be alone, I should have a gun for protection, and without further thought I immediately went looking for a pawn shop. When I found one, I walked in and without the slightest trepidation announced that I would like to buy a gun. The man gave me a "You got to be kidding" look, and mumbled something under his breath as he walked away. I thought that he was going to get a gun to sell me. Instead he came back empty-handed and told me to follow him to his home where I could get one. When we got there, I was greeted by cops. I couldn't understand why. I hadn't done anything wrong. They asked me why I needed a gun. I told them that I was going to New York alone and felt that I needed a gun for protection. They told me emphatically that a gun was illegal, and that it was not a good idea to go to New York alone. That advice went in one ear and out the other. I WAS GOING! I needed to go. This compulsion was so great that when I did get to New York, I didn't want to stop there. I wanted to go to Europe, the Middle East — the farther away, the better. If I had the opportunity, I would have gone on without a moment's hesitation. In one phone conversation with my parents I told them of this intention. However, God was watching over me in answer to all the prayers that were sent up to Him on my behalf. Without His protection I would most certainly have met with disaster. One psychiatrist predicted as much to my mom when she called to ask him what to do as I had gone to New York. "Don't worry," he said, "you will find her either in a hospital, a jail, or . . ." He stopped short of saying in a morgue, but that's the thinking he projected. His words alarmed my parents as nothing else had done.

I went back to my apartment and frittered the rest of the day away. That same evening I took a long shower. Even though I had made reservations at the Waldorf Astoria, I remember thinking that I had better take a good shower because it might be a long time before I'd get another one. This feeling or premonition became stark reality.

At about 10:00 p.m. I had the car loaded with my clothes, blankets, my stereo cassette player, my two Bibles, and everything else I thought I might need. I grabbed my kitty, stopped at Domino's for a pizza to take along, and we were on our way. What an exciting adventure!

I hadn't driven more than 25 miles or so when I felt tired, pulled to the side of the road in a small town and lay down for a rest. It did not strike me as odd that I would leave my comfortable apartment and bed to drive just a few miles. Nor did I think it was odd to leave so late at night. This is what I did on all my wild trips — leave at night, drive a few miles and then sleep in the car. Perhaps due to the inner restlessness I experienced and the racing thoughts that I felt, I just couldn't wait until morning to leave. I went to sleep petting my kitty.

June 25, 1983

I didn't wake up this Saturday morning until it was getting light. I felt great! I put a cassette into my tape recorder and started talking. I felt the need to talk, talk, talk. I talked about my inner desires, about God, my goals and everything and anything that came to mind. I played my music tapes over and over. All this kept me occupied until I reached

Minneapolis. It was afternoon and I hadn't eaten anything because I just wasn't hungry anymore. This was a change, for in the winter when I was sleeping so much, I could eat all the time. Now I felt too excited to eat.

In spite of my great self-confidence, I still had some concern for my personal security, and I decided to go to the police station to get a can of mace for protection. I don't know how I found the police station, but I did. I told them about my trip and the need for protection. I'm sure they were wondering about me, but they told me I should be able to buy mace at any truck stop.

I left the police station and had gone a little ways when I suddenly realized that my kitty was not in the car. To continue on without my cat was unthinkable. I turned around and retraced my route calling, "Kitty, kitty," out the window of my car. I was becoming more and more agitated when miraculously I heard a loud screeching, "Meow!" coming from up in a tree. What a relief! It took a while, but I got my precious kitty, and we were off again. My poor little kitty, I realize now, was neglected. I can't think about that because it makes me feel so bad. At the time I thought that I was taking such good care of him.

I stopped at wayside rest areas mostly and while at one of these stops, I met three truck drivers from Minnesota. I was talking to everyone now — jabber, jabber, jabber. I told them that I was going to New York, and they suggested that I follow them as they were going that way. Another big relief. This way I wouldn't have to rely on the maps I had purchased. When they stopped to sleep for a few hours or eat, I did the same. When they smoked pot and gave me some, I smoked pot with them. They slept in their trucks and I slept in my car. It was hot and uncomfortable, but I kept thinking of my destination. These truck drivers did not try to take advantage of me. I was becoming more manic, and it never ocurred to me that there was any danger in being alone. I wasn't afraid of anyone or anything. I had lost my imagination and my ability to foresee possible dangers. While driving, I continued to talk into my tape recorder and I listened to my favorite song. This, together with my kitty and the stops, kept me busy until we reached Pennsylvania where the truck drivers and I parted company.

June 26, 1983

It was Sunday and I decided to stop at a wayside lookout point to take in the view before going into New York. Here I met two guys, Hassan and Kose. Kose was rather scruffy looking, but Hassan was better groomed and spoke much better English. They said that they were Iranians. They were very friendly and offered me some cocaine they were snorting. Not giving it a second thought, I tried to snort it the way they did, but nothing happened. Perhaps I was already so high from my illness that it did not affect me at all. They offered to show me around New York City. Boy, I certainly was game for that. I followed them to Jersey City to a Holiday Inn where they got a room.

While there, I decided to call home. Mom answered the phone, and I proceeded to tell her that I was having a great time at the lake. She believed me. As I hung up the receiver I chuckled to myself for there, on the table right in front of me, was the leftover cocaine. I could not help thinking how flipped-out my family would be if they knew where I really was and what I was doing!

I had loved my family, but the love was changing to a feeling of ambivalence. They hadn't done or said anything to cause the change — it was just that everything seemed to be changing. My whole outlook on life was taking a sinister turn. This diabolical, insidious illness was robbing me of my love for my family, my values and all that I had held so dear. Living my life to please and be used by God had been so important to me. I found it hard to understand why I should have been cursed with an illness that made me do things that, as a Christian, I would never have wanted to do. I can now easily understand why come people feel that mental illness is due to demon possession. It certainly has all the evil side-effects, but it is not demon possession. Lithium stabilizes the chemical imbalance. My belief in God was, and still is, real. I never lost my faith even though I couldn't live up to it during my manic spells. I can only conclude that the love of God protected me while I was so vulnerable.

However, as my illness worsened, my beliefs became distorted. I felt that, in some wonderful and mysterious way, God was going to use me to help all the poor people of the world, especially those in New York. I believed that God had revealed to me the imminent destruction of this large and heavily populated city. I was to be His extra-special servant. As this delusion mushroomed, I began to feel that I had to stay in New York to warn people about the impending disaster.

The two Iranian's brought me back to the present when they grabbed my arm and said, "Let's go!" We first drove to a Jewish restaurant located near Greenwich Village. There I ordered lamb for the first time and found it very good. This was my first meal since I had left home. After eating, we drove around New York, hitting all the *low* spots. We also spent some time in Washington Square Park. We didn't get back to the Holiday Inn until almost dawn.

I went straight to bed with my clothes on. Hassan promptly fell asleep, but Kose, the jerk, kept trying to entice me into his bed. "Psst, psst, come here! Come on! Psst, psst!" I had no intention of complying with his wishes, but he kept up his coaxing. "Psst, psst, come here!" he repeated. When he suddenly got out of bed, I knew it was time to make a hasty getaway. I jumped out of bed yelling at Hassan to wake up as I ran out the door to the lobby. I stayed there until Hassan came to tell me that it was safe to come back to get my things. Hassan even apologized for what had happened.

Chapter 6

THE MINNESOTA STRIP

(Cindy) June 27, 1983

As I left the Holiday Inn, a gray, drizzly day greeted me. The traffic was terrible, and I wasn't sure just which highway to take but that didn't dampen my spirits or deter me. Everyone seemed to be driving so fast and recklessly. I couldn't see how I was driving! I could see New York, and I didn't want to pass it by, so I managed to maneuver off the freeway, which had eight or ten lanes, onto another busy highway that looked promising. It led me to the middle of the city.

It was raining harder now, and the streets were so narrow and filled with cars whizzing by, with people everywhere. I was in a daze. It was hard to see the stoplights as they were positioned differently and appeared smaller. Suddenly, I flew forward as I heard the crunch of metal! "What's happened?!" I said out loud. Someone had rammed into the side of my car. The other driver jumped out, angrily waving his arms and yelling. I rolled down my window, and he read me the riot act. I gave him my name and all the particulars without any objection. It was my fault. I had run a light. Oh, well, even though the side of my car was crunched, it didn't hamper driving. The other car was undamaged, so I just drove off. Another close call, but I was undaunted by it all.

"Where is the Waldorf Astoria?" I called to a pedestrian. He told me it was close by and pointed to where I should go, but I couldn't find it. I ended up parking my car on the top floor of the Port Authority, the bus station where girls are picked up by pimps as they come off the buses. It was the notorious Minnesota Strip! I did not realize that at the time. In my state of mind, it would not have bothered me anyway.

I didn't remember the books I had read about this area of New York, and the great concern I had for the poor girls who ended up here.

Right now I needed to find the Waldorf Astoria. I looked up at all the marquees advertising sex. One caught my eye, The Seduction of Cindy! I was already shivering in the rain, but that sent chills down my spine. God wants me here, I thought to myself, and I'm going to do whatever He wants me to do!

A policeman gave me clear directions to the Waldorf Astoria. As I was shouldering my way through the crowds of people toward Waldorf, a big, ugly Hispanic, wearing faded red sweat pants and a dirty T-shirt, started walking with me. That didn't scare me. He looked like one of those poor souls that God wanted me to help.

I offered him a cigarette — great way to help! We walked on to the Waldorf where, for reasons no longer clear to me, I canceled the reservation. I had not planned to do that — my plan was to stay at the swank hotel. We sat down in the beautiful, luxurious lounge with it's elegant furniture, white plush carpet and huge grand piano. A violinist was entertaining the guests, and I was enchanted by it all. I ordered drinks for my new friend, Cortez, and myself. He was uneasy and fidgety, urging me to leave. "Hey, man, come on. I'll take you to a place where the drinks are cheap!" I objected, "No, I want to be here. Isn't it gorgeous! I've got plenty of money." This was a really smart thing to say to someone who obviously had nothing but the clothes on his back. Actually, I had about $150 left.

When we left the hotel, Cortez stuck to me like glue. We were walking down 42nd Street. In my manic state of mind, I was smiling and friendly to everyone as long as they didn't cross me in any way. I was also extremely irritable. I learned later that at such times the pupils in my eyes became dilated, even in broad daylight.

Cortez learned that I had a car, so he asked me if I would take him to his sister's house. "Sure, I've got the car parked at Port Authority," I chirped. When we got to the car, he tried to get me to sneak out without paying, but I didn't want to do that. When the attendant said it would be $10, I was rather put out as it had been for such a short time. Oh, well, I had the money, so I paid, and we were off speeding through the traffic.

Cortez started telling me about himself. I had been unflappable by all he said until he told me that he had committed three murders and went into detail about the circumstances. This finally scared me. He said that he was on parole. I hadn't forgotten what murder meant, so I knew that I had to get rid of him. I pulled to the side of the road that led to what looked like a school. I then told him that I had to go to the bathroom. Instead I ran a couple of blocks to the other side of the building, so he wouldn't see me use a phone. I called the cops and told them about Cortez and that I was afraid of him. They could not have cared less. I hung up the receiver, not knowing what to do next. It was still raining and miserable. I tried to hail down a cab as I thought they could help me. Five or six went by before one stopped. I told him about Cortez, but he didn't want to get involved. He dropped me off, and I gave him the two dollars that I had in my purse.

I could see that my car was still there. I ran to the car and found it in an absolute mess. Everything was scattered here and there. I had left my door open and the keys in the ignition. Where is my kitty? "Kitty, Kitty, Kitty," I cried. Out from under the seat a little head appeared. What a relief! I hadn't lost my kitty. My stereo and tapes were gone. I was sure that my money had been stolen, as I couldn't find it in my frantic search. Unexplainably, I calmed down, shrugged my shoulders and thought, "Great, I'm in New York without a red cent. Oh well, God will take care of me. At least I have my car." The keys were still dangling in the ignition. Cortez had gone for which I was now thankful.

I turned the car around and headed back to 42nd Street, like a moth drawn to light. I don't know why I was drawn to that terrible place. I don't even know how I found my way back there. This time I went to the parking lot at the Ramada Inn. I had to park in the basement where it was hot and closed-in, but I wasn't going to pay $10 again at Port Authority. I soon learned that was the going rate for parking. I had no money, so I guessed this would be my home until I could find a job. I would take my kitty out for walks. I took him with me to Blimpey's where I asked for some food for myself and my cat. The manager was very kind, giving me a bagel with cheese and some milk which I shared with my kitty. It never once occurred to me that I should call home for money or go home. I had a mission to fulfill for God. This was the only thought that was really clear to me. I was not going home even though this illness had now reduced me to begging. I am appalled by this now. I realize now that many of the people walking the streets are mentally ill, and my heart goes out to them. Their lives are totally miserable, and there is no one to help or seemingly care. Without the love and help of my family, who never gave up on me, I would probably still be on the streets or more likely dead.

There was a Kodak camera shop right next to Blimpey's, so I stopped there. Here I met two men who gave me all kinds of compliments. The short one with kinky hair was Jewish. He said, "Have you ever done any modeling? You could easily be a model! Would you like to make lots of money?" "Yah, I'd like that, but I'd settle for a job as a waitress. Do you know of any such job?" I asked. "Maybe," they answered. They were so friendly and seemed genuinely interested in helping me. Their names were Judah and Franklin. They told me to come back at 11:00 p.m. closing time, and we could talk about it at a bar.

I came back at closing time, and they took me to a bar. Afterwards, Franklin dropped Judah and me at a house in Queen's. Judah introduced me to his sister from Israel who was going back there shortly. That really got me thinking. I would love to go to Israel, God's country. Maybe I could go with her. It was getting late and Judah had plans for me. I was in such a fog that I couldn't seem to figure anything out.

His advances were a surprise to me. When I resisted, he left me alone. I had lost almost all of my inhibitions, but one thing I would not do was have sex with anyone! So far that was still a sin to me.

Tuesday, June 28, 1983

The next morning, I had my first shower since leaving home. It was a slimy, tiny shower stall, but that shower was unforgettable. I didn't have clean clothes to put on, but I felt so much better. I went with Judah on the subway train back to 42nd Street; he to his job and me to roaming the streets.

I walked up to people, asked their names, addresses and telephone numbers, and sometimes made arrangements to meet them in the park. I thought each person had a connection of importance in my life. I kept going back to Blimpey's for handouts. I also got steak-a-bubs and other food from people with food carts which they gave me willingly. I took my cat to the park for walks, taking down names and addresses all along the way.

I went back to my car when it got late enough. I would like to watch the black people break dancing during the night, and there were so many exciting things going on in the streets at night. I eventually went back to my car to sleep. Sometime during the night a guy knocked on my window. I had locked my doors, and did not open the door at his persistence. I think that scared me a little. Eventually he left. Having a cat was a comfort to me. I didn't feel quite so alone.

When I woke up after sleeping in my car, I felt hot, sticky and had an inner restlessness that was making me more hyper and miserable. As weeks and months went by this inner restlessness and racing thoughts became sheer torture. I hurried to the Ramada Inn's bathroom to get washed up. It was about 6 or 7:00 a.m. when I decided to call home. My dad answered the phone. His first words were, "Cindy, we're so glad you called, but how come you are up so early?" "Oh, we got up early to go out to the lake," I lied. I don't know when my dad had been so full of questions. His next one was, "Where are you calling from?" I had to think fast to come up with a believable answer. "I'm calling from a gas station." "What's the name of it?" he asked. "Amoco Station," I shot back. By now Mom was on the phone too. I tried to stop the conversation, but I didn't want to hang up on them because then they would know something was wrong. I promised to call again soon. This got me off the hook. I hung up the phone and headed down the street to Blimpey's for another handout for me and my kitty. I was becoming a regular there.

While there, I met a black man named Johnny. He seemed nice. He was friendly, so I started talking to him and telling him every little thing, including the fact that my money had been stolen the first day that I came to New York. He said, "Hey, I'll fix you up, so you can get some money. Don't worry. I'll make the arrangements and be back here tonight with my plan. O.K?" It sounded good to me. I can't believe how gullible I was. I thought maybe he was going to get me a job as a waitress or clerk or something like that. That would be great. This illness was making me stupid. I just couldn't think straight.

There were people gathered on the street corners, preaching, handing out tracts, selling things, sitting or standing along the street begging. I decided to listen to the Muslims preach their religion. I was hyper, so I couldn't stand there long, and I sure didn't agree with what they were preaching. I went up to one of the bearded men, dressed in his native garb and said, "I don't agree with what you are saying!" He looked at me with such piercing evil eyes that I didn't dare say another word. I got out of there in a hurry.

I came back to Blimpey's in the evening, and so did Johnny. He said, "I've got it all arranged. Come with me." I followed him with anticipation. We took the subway to some out-of-the-way place. When we got out, I couldn't help but notice how deserted and dark it was. We walked a ways to a shabby building, climbed two flights of stairs and entered a dingy little room. There was a bed, a dresser and clothes strewn all over. Now, at last, he was ready to tell me his plan. "I've talked to a guy. I told him you are a prostitute and how good looking you are, so he is coming over here. I know he has lots of money. When he takes his pants off, I'll grab his billfold, and we'll split with it!"

I was feeling claustrophobic by now in this little suffocating room. The mental fog must have cleared a little because this didn't seem right. However, I felt safe with this big black man that I had just met. I thought that he would protect me. He insisted, "Take off your clothes. That is the only way we can fool him into believing you really are a prostitute!" I took my shoes off and started unbuttoning my blouse when suddenly I was overwhelmed with a sense of danger. "Oh God, help me! I've got to get out of here," I prayed. I grabbed my purse, forgetting my shoes in my hurry to get away. I ran down the stairs and out the door to what seemed the darkest, most desolate street in the world. There was no one around. I ran as fast as I could in the direction I thought we had come. I didn't have money for the bus fare, so I asked two or three stragglers for money. I hurriedly collected the 75 cents I needed. When I got on the bus, I felt safe. Johnny didn't try to stop me. I believe now that he was one of the mentally ill people walking the streets of New York. I saw him a day or two later, and he said that he felt bad about the whole thing.

When I reached 42nd Street, I headed for my car. I needed shoes and fortunately I had another pair along. Unexplainably, I felt very ambitious. I decided to clean my car. Up to this point I had done absolutely nothing constructive. When I was digging around in my suitcase, I just couldn't believe my eyes! There was my money, right where it was supposed to be. I quickly counted it. One hundred dollars, the exact amount. Cortez hadn't stolen my money after all. If this money hadn't been stolen, maybe the little magnetic container with about fifty dollars might still be in the trunk. Sure enough, there it was, money intact. I felt rich! I immediately rushed to Blimpey's to tell whoever was working there about my good fortune. I told everybody everything. After having something to eat and paying for it this time, I went to the car to sleep.

Thursday, June 30, 1983

The next morning I woke up to the heat and the now familiar pungent smells of food sold in the streets, to the noise and to the masses of people. People everywhere. Where were they all going? Some, like myself, weren't going anywhere. I kept meeting some of the same people over and over. I often saw Cortez, with or without my stereo. If I saw him in time, I would try to avoid him. I didn't trust him after what he had told me about himself. He complained that he didn't like that I didn't trust him. He'd ask me to go places with him. One day I saw him at the park. I walked over to a cop and when I turned around, Cortez had disappeared.

The manager of Blimpey's had sort of taken me under his wing, so I listened to him when he warned me to beware of certain individuals. One person that he warned me about was a man named Jesus. I had seen him at Blimpey's a few times, and he tried to talk to me. I avoided him because I was scared of him. He was an evil and dangerous man. His name was unforgettable. He was to take an interest in me a few days later.

It was about 3:00 or so in the morning, and I was still walking up and down 42nd Street. I wasn't looking forward to the hot, stuffy car, so I wasn't in a hurry. Suddenly, I heard the clopping of horse's hooves on the pavement. I turned around and there was a young guy heading for home after a long day of giving carriage rides to tourists. He saw me and yelled, "Hop on. I'll give you a ride!" I immediately obliged. This was fun. He was friendly. I learned that he was French and 17 years old. He also invited me to his apartment. Great, I wouldn't have to sleep in the hot, stuffy car. He, of course, was no different from all the others. When he realized that I was not at all interested in what he had in mind for me, he told me to go in no uncertain terms. "Get out!" I begged, "Can't I sleep on your couch or the floor until morning?" "No, get out!" he yelled in anger. I left, walking so very slowly to the car where at least the cat was happy to see me. It still never occurred to me that I could and should go home. It seemed I would not be as manic or high at night because I would sometimes feel so alone.

In addition to writing down names and phone numbers of people who, I imagined, would have a connection with me in the future, initials began to take on special meaning to me. J, JB, and JD were extra-special. These letters had spiritual significance to me. I named my kitty John Boy because of this new revelation. My thinking was completely confused. Nothing was as I thought. Being dirty was bothering me less and less.

Friday, July 1, 1983

This morning I woke up to a new day which was a blur of sameness. I took my car out of the Ramada parking, using my last $30. I drove to Port Authority and parked it there again. I ran into Lawyer Jim often at Port Authority. He had given me his card and each time I saw him, he would remind me that he was my friend and was there to help anytime. He seemed nice enough even though he was bossy. I guess he was the one who told me to bring my car to Port Authority. He was a big, black man with huge lips, wearing dark clothes. I was not put off by his appearance; in fact, he was to keep in contact with me for months. There was a time that I believed he was the only friend that I had in this world. I was a hairbreadth away from falling prey to this unscrupulous man.

I frittered away the day and slept in my car again. It was not quite as hot and stuffy on the top floor of this parking ramp.

Saturday, July 2, 1983

I woke up this morning with a purpose in mind. I decided to make New York my home. It was my sixth day in New York, and now I wanted a place to sleep, other than my car. I wanted a job because I didn't have a red cent to my name. A job and a home. That's what I need! With that in mind I walked to the park, went up to a cop and told him that I needed a place to sleep. He told me that he would send me to someone who could give me some help. He wrote out the name and address of a lady who was a counselor.

It took me a while, but I found her office. After answering her many questions, she suggested that I go to the Covenant House, a home for people under 21 years of age who had nowhere else to go. I was under 21, had no place else to go, so I qualified. She assured me that she would make arrangements for me to get in there. "Now I have a home in New York! This is going to be my city. Wow!"

On my way to the Covenant House I met three men taking their food carts home. As per usual I took down their names, addresses and telephone numbers. One of the men, an Egyptian, asked me where I was going. I told him that I was on my way to the Covenant House, that I was broke and everything else that I could think of. I talked nonstop. He interrupted. "Would you like a job?" If I was ecstatic before, now I was delirious! I not only would have a place to stay, but I had a job as well. "Of course, I want a job!" I screeched. He said that he would buy me an ice cream cart and made me promise to meet him the next day. I would be there for sure. He could depend on me. Then I continued on my way to the Covenant House.

When I got to the Covenant House, I was greeted by very friendly people. They talked to me for a while, asking questions to learn about me after which they read the rules to me. I don't remember them, but I was to learn about the curfew the hard way. They signed me in. I was told that there were no beds left, but that I could sleep on the floor, and that I would be safe there. I breathed a sigh of relief, but I could not relax. I went to the street and made my way back to 42nd Street. Blimpey's was my destination. There I met another Egyptian named Phillipi. He bragged that he had a band and he was planning to tour the Middle East. My ears perked up. I quickly informed him that I played the piano. To my great delight, he said that he needed a keyboard player. He invited me to his house to try out the keyboard and to see all his band equipment.

When I got to his house, I decided to call home. Now that things were going so good for me I wanted to tell my folks where I really was. I used my trusty credit card as I had been doing every day — not just calling home, but to Kelly and many others.

It was about 4:00 in the afternoon when I made the call. Jeff answered the phone. I excitedly told him that I was in New York! When he heard that, he immediately got on my case. Soon Dad was on the phone, and they both were giving me a bad time. They couldn't accept the fact that I wanted to live in New York. They kept on and on until I got so upset that I forgot to tell them that I had a place to stay and a job. They said that Mom wouldn't be able to take that kind of news. I asked to talk to her, but they said that she wouldn't be home until 7:00 p.m. I had had enough harassment from them. I cut them off by saying I would call back at seven to talk to Mom. Then I hung up the receiver. I was so angry and upset that I stomped out of Phillipi's house, forgetting even what I was doing there. Jeff and Dad had spoiled a terrific day. Why couldn't they understand that I had a mission in New York?!

At about 7:00 p.m. I went to the Ramada Inn to call Mom. When she answered the phone, she sounded just fine. I didn't think that Dad and Jeff knew what they were talking about. In our conversation she told me that I should be taking lithium because the doctor had diagnosed me as having a bipolar disorder. She read the symptoms and asked me to go to Bellevue Hospital and get lithium. I couldn't relate to what she was saying, but I told her that I would maybe get some lithium. I knew there wasn't anything wrong with me, but I did actually

...ppointment at Bellevue Hospital. Again I forgot to ...out my new home and job.

...ked back to the Covenant House. I talked to some ...re. One was a black girl who was full of fun, and I liked her. The two of us decided that we would get an apartment together as soon as we made enough money. One of the girls liked my leather purse, so I poured all the contents of my purse into a dufflebag that I had and gave her my purse. I slept on the floor that night with the others.

Sunday, July 3, 1983

It was almost noon when I woke up at the Covenant House. I must have relaxed more there to make it possible for me to sleep so long. I got up and had something to eat. After eating, I asked if I could use the phone. I showed the people in charge my telephone credit card. They were more than happy to let me use the phone. I called home to tell them that I had a home and a job and was so thrilled about how everything was working out for me.

When I told Mom that I was at the Covenant House, she didn't believe me. To prove to her that I was telling the truth, I asked one of the attendants to talk to her. They talked so long that I was getting agitated. I wanted to tell Mom about my job. When I got back on the line, I went on and on about my new job. I would be selling ice cream right downtown in front of Macy's. I was so excited. After hanging up the receiver, I took off to meet the Egyptian to start my job.

Sure enough, there he was with the ice cream cart. It was big and heavy and hard to push, but I didn't mind. The Egyptian said that I would get a commission, so the more I sold, the more money I would make. It was a stifling hot day, so ice cream sales were very good. I stayed across the street from Macy's. We worked for about 3 1/2 hours. My boss and two others had their carts close by, so I kept on until they said it was time to quit. We pulled our carts back to where they were stored. He paid me $30 commission and asked me to come back the next day, July 4th. I promised faithfully to be back the next day and went on my merry way feeling so good about the money I had earned.

I went to my car for my kitty at Port Authority. When I got there, who was there to greet me with a big smile, but Lawyer Jim. He was so interested in my welfare and acted as though he was very much concerned about me. I, of course, told him about my job and the $30 that I had earned. He seemed happy that I had taken his advice and brought my car to this place.

After getting my cat, John Boy, and walking the stairway to second floor, a guy came along side me and starting talking. It was Jesus. He claimed that I needn't be afraid of him since he was Jesus. He also said that he would help me and do things for me. I had been warned about this low life while at Blimpey's, so I started running down the escalator as fast as I could. He was running right behind me. When I got to the bottom of the escalator, there were two cops by the doors. I ran up to them and asked for help, but they said there was nothing they could to help. I screamed and swore at them and ran across the street to another cop. Jesus was right behind.

Breathlessly, I told them that I was scared of this creep. This cop was nice, but said, "There isn't much I can do but hold him a few minutes, so that you can get away." He grabbed Jesus, and I took off as fast as I could running across the street from Blimpey's.

I tore by a man leaning against a fence. He called to me saying, "I saw you were being chased. If you are scared, I'll walk with you for a while." I stopped running. That sounded fine to me. No one had warned me about this guy. His name was Perez, I learned. He took me to a French Cafe and bought me something to eat. The cat was drinking water out of my glass, and the people in the next booth complained about it. That didn't bother me a bit. I giggled and let the cat continue drinking. This was not like me at all. Nothing I was doing these days was like me! In the course of the one-sided conversation,

I told Perez about my car and how expensive it was to park in New York. He immediately responded with the suggestion that I park at his house at Woodside. Was that ever good news! He said, "It won't cost you anything, and it can be parked there as long as you want." I couldn't believe it. This was too good to be true! I jumped up and said, "Come on, let's go to Port Authority for my car. I made $30 today. That should be enough to get my car out."

When we got to Port Authority, who was there to greet us, but big, black Lawyer Jim. He wanted to know what I was doing. I told him that Perez said that I could park my car at his house for nothing. Jim was not at all pleased when he heard that. He said, "How can you trust this guy? You just met him. He'll probably swindle you out of your car." Perez heard what he was saying, but didn't argue. I wanted my car out of this place, and I didn't listen to Lawyer Jim. I wonder what HE had in mind for my car and me! We marched past him, and I paid my $30 to get my car out. Broke again, but I would be earning more the next day, I comforted myself.

Perez told me where to drive, and we drove and drove. I remember looking up at the Statue of Liberty as we drove by. Finally, we got to Woodside. We came to a crummy section and parked by a shabby green house. Perez told me to park my car on the edge of the gravel road in front of this house. We got out of the car and walked in.

There was a big beautiful calico cat. "A friend for my kitty!" I exclaimed. I put my little tiger kitty down next to the white cat, and I thought that they liked each other right away. This was terrific. Then I noticed Perez's roommate, a huge man with a shaved head, an earring hanging in one ear, wearing a jean jacket with a knife in full view on his belt. He seemed friendly enough, so I wasn't scared of him. I was only scared of people about whom I had been warned. Perez said that they would give me a ride back to the Covenant House. I took some clothes and things from the car and stuffed them into a bag. I left my cat and car there, and got into his roommate's pickup to head back.

On the way we stopped at a bar. It was dark and noisy in there. I trusted these strangers, so I followed them down the stairs to a dark, but quiet room. Here people were drinking and smoking pot. I don't know how long we were there. I had completely forgotten about the curfew at the Covenant House. I had even forgotten about the Covenant House. It was in the wee hours of the morning that they decided to leave. They dropped me off at the Covenant House.

When I rang the bell to get in, I was greeted with the words, "It is after curfew, so you will not be allowed to stay here anymore! Get your things and leave." "Can't I just stay here until morning? I don't have any place to go," I begged. The answer was, "No, you broke curfew; you should have thought of that before coming in at this time of the night." Now I can understand the reason for their harsh treatment, but at the time I was devastated. They thought that I was a prostitute and was deliberately breaking the rules, and this could not be tolerated, I suppose. I went in, picked up my belongings, stuffed them into a garbage bag and went to the streets. Where will I sleep? I don't even have my car now. I have to go back for my car!!

I couldn't remember where it was, except that it was somewhere in Woodside. I hurried back to Port Authority to put my clothes in one of the lockers. I had become acquainted with Bruce, the only Caucasian who worked there. He informed me that there were no lockers available, but that he would find me an old suitcase and would put it in the back room. Then I left, determined to somehow find my car. I had Perez's telephone number, but it was just a phone service, so he wouldn't get the message until the next day. I hadn't thought to get the Woodside address. I was always getting addresses, but I didn't get the one address that I needed. I had to find my car.

I kept asking until I found a bus that went to Woodside. I was getting good at asking and begging. When I got to Woodside, I was completely disoriented. I had no idea where to go from there. I walked into Tower's Diner, a small corner cafe, not knowing what else to do. I didn't have any money to order anything, so I just sat there. Soon a guy sat down by me at the counter and started talking. He ordered something for me to eat. I told him of my plight, and he said that he would take me around the side streets to look for my car. I gratefully got into his car, but instead of looking for my car, he stopped at a motel. When I saw the motel sign, my reaction was, "Oh, good, now I can sleep." I was naive and gullible beyond belief. I just couldn't think clearly or rationally about anything.

His name was Nick. He was dark with a small mustache. With pride in his voice, he told me that he was Greek. I said that I was Norwegian. He had bought some beer to bring along which I helped him drink until I felt sick. I let him kiss me, but when he wanted to go further, I said emphatically, "I'm not that kind of girl!" He said something like, "You could have fooled me." He became very quiet and sullen, but got up to leave without making an issue of it. He must have felt sorry for me because as he left, he threw $10 on the dresser saying, "You may need that." I thought he was so nice. I slept until the sun shone through the windows the next morning.

Monday, July 4, 1983

July 4th, the big, exciting day that I had been waiting for was here! I suddenly remembered that I was supposed to sell ice cream, so I jumped out of bed. I didn't have time to take a shower in my hurry to find my way back to my home, 42nd Street.

I paid for my bus fare with the $10 Nick left me. As I was hurrying down 42nd Street, I met my Egyptian boss. He waved and said, "You'll be there for me, won't you? I bought an ice cream cart just for you!" I said, "I sure will!" I didn't have to rush since I didn't have to work yet, so I made my way through the crowds of people to Blimpey's. I was feeling so great; euphoric or ecstatic might better describe how I felt. This was the life. There was so much excitement in the air. It was the Fourth of July! Home or my folks didn't enter my mind.

As I was walking happily along, here comes Cortez. Today he is angry. He snarled at me. "Why didn't you trust me? I hate when people don't trust me!" I smarted off to him. Then he hauled off and slapped me across the face as hard as he could and growled, "You're going with me to the beach today!" I gasped, but kept my cool. "O.K., I'll go with you to the beach," I lied. He continued walking with me, and I was looking for a way to get away from him. As we walked by a motel, I dashed through the door with Cortez right behind, ran up to the clerk yelling, "Call the security guard. This man is harassing me!" At first she hesitated, but when she reached for the receiver of the phone, Cortez disappeared. My face was still smarting, so I decided to call home. I needed to hear my Mom's comforting voice right now. Mom was so glad that I was at Covenant House that I didn't tell her that I had been kicked out. There were glimmers of clearer thinking every once in awhile. When I hung up the phone, I felt better.

I never did get to the ice cream cart. I was still full of energy, but I couldn't focus on any one thing. The job that had been so important to me was forgotten. The afternoon was spent talking to people, giving out cigarettes and walking. Later, that evening, I was at Blimpey's again. Someone walked up to me and said, "Your brothers are looking for you!" I was shocked, but skeptical. I had told them never to do that, or I would disappear for good. "How do you know that?" I asked. He then described my brothers to a T. He also said that they had a family picture that they were showing around, and I was in that picture. I got so upset! I had to find out if it was true. I just couldn't believe that Lonnie and Jeff were in New York looking for me. He had to be mistaken. I'm never leaving New York. They'll never get me to go home!

I went straight to the phone and called home. I stated emphatically, "Lonnie and Jeff are here looking for me, aren't they?!" Mom said they weren't, but I suspected that she was covering up. I then called Lonnie's house. Jan answered, so I asked to talk to Lonnie. She said that he was not at home right then. I hung up the phone getting more uneasy by the minute. I called Jeff's apartment. Same story. Carla answered and said that Jeff was out on a job, so I couldn't talk to him right then. I felt sick. I knew that it must be true. They were here looking for me. The next minute I was on the phone to Mom again, and said, "I KNOW Lon and Jeff are here, so don't deny it." I shocked myself by what I said next. "Tell them that I'll meet them in the morning at 10:00 a.m. at the Ramada Inn at 8th and 42nd Street." I hung up the phone puzzling over what I had just said. Why did I say that? I don't want to see them; yet I want to see them. I hate my family; yet I love my family. Things were so mixed up.

I went out again to do some serious walking, but there were so many people that it was hard to walk. I don't know how long I had been walking, but I ended up at Port Authority. I told Bruce that I had to find my car. He said, "I get off at midnight. Just wait around, and I'll take you to your car." Good! I needed my car. I needed a place to sleep.

At midnight I was there, and we took off to look for my car. We drove and drove, but instead of ending up at Woodside he stopped at a motel. Same story. My reaction, "Great, now I'll get some sleep." It seemed like a replay of the night before. When he found that I was not the least bit interested, he was disgusted and left. In the morning I found $10 on the dresser. He must have felt sorry for me just like Nick. I was so grateful. I believe that God was protecting and taking care of me in this desperate situation of being sick and alone in this huge city.

Tuesday, July 5, 1983

This morning I woke up with a start. I remembered that I was supposed to meet Lonnie and Jeff at 10:00 a.m. I jumped out of bed and got ready as fast as I could, which wasn't that fast. I just had to take a shower. I soon learned that I had left my shoes in Bruce's car, so I was barefoot again. The sidewalk burned my feet as I walked and walked in search of shoes. I don't know why it mattered to me because nothing else seemed to matter, but I didn't want to meet my brothers without shoes. After walking for blocks and what seemed hours, I found a store that sold shoes for a reasonable price. I found some sandals that cost $12 , but they sold them to me for $10. I, then, decided to call home to say that I would be late. I don't know what good I thought that would do. Anyway, I called, and Mom seemed overjoyed that I had called. After hanging up, I collected enough money from people for the bus ride back to 42nd Street. I tried to hurry on to the Ramada Inn to meet my brothers, but I was in a daze; so I'm sure it took a while. I still had to stop and get a name and phone number here and there along the way.

I finally made it to the Ramada, and there were my brothers. I didn't feel happy or sad to see them. I was numb. They were so happy to see me. They hugged me and told me they loved me, but I didn't hug them back. I wasn't going back home with them and that was for sure! A private investigator was with them. He was full of fun and joked with me. I told them that I had to hurry because I had an appointment with a black man who was going to get me a job. They wanted to come along, and I said they could if they would stay far enough away, so the guy wouldn't know they were with me. Afterwards, the private investigator, Tony, told my brothers that he was a pimp. He knew better than to tell ME that.

I dread to think what would have happened to me had I been on the streets another week. I was being watched by evil men, who like vultures, were waiting for the opportune time to pounce. I was becoming more ill, more vulnerable because of impaired judgment as each day went by, so my brothers came in the nick of time.

Chapter 7

BROTHERLY LOVE

(Brother Jeff) Monday, July 4, 1983

There were four of us in our apartment around 11:00 a.m. on the 4th of July when the phone rang. My brother, Lon, and his wife, Jan, had come to make plans to spend the evening with Carla and me at the local fair. Louise Mandrell, a celebrity worth hearing we decided, would be performing at the grandstand. Maybe it would take our minds off our problems for a little while. Lon and I were still reeling from all that had been going on in our lives. With the loss of our family businesses, the loss of our jobs, and our little sister somewhere in New York City, sick and alone, our lives had become nightmares.

I lifted the receiver — it was Mom, all bent out of shape. "Jeff, will you and Lonnie go to New York and try to find Cindy? She has left the Covenant House, and something just has to be done. I know you have plans for tonight, but I'm getting desperate!"

"Mom!," I interrupted, "Mom, we'll go! WE'LL GO! We may not be able to go today since it's a holiday and on such short notice, but we'll try."

"Try right away. We have the $5,000 we have been saving that you will have to take along."

"O.K., we'll call for reservations right away. Hang in there Mom, we'll find her." I hung up the phone thinking, how in the world can we find Cindy in New York City? But we had to try. Lonnie and I made some quick decisions. Although Lonnie had a phobia about flying, he did not mention it. I called the airlines in Grand Forks and, miraculously, there was a flight out at 3:00 p.m. Lonnie called Bob, a deputy sheriff, asking him for help and suggestions. Bob knew a private investigator in New York and would contact him that we were heading out there. He would get his phone number and give it to Mom, so that when we called home, she could give it to us. He also suggested that we take a family picture along for identification. We then threw a few things into a suitcase, sped to our parents home for the money, and broke the speed limit all the way to the airport with the tires on Lonnie's small Trans Am rubbing from the weight of four people. Our wives were very patient and understanding about our going, but at the rate we were going, they feared we wouldn't make it to the airport, much less New York. We did make it, just in time. We boarded the plane and were off, not having a clue how we would find Cindy. What would the next few days bring?!! We landed at Kennedy Airport about 7:00 that evening. We got off the plane, picked up our luggage, went outside, not sure what to do. We saw a long line of buses, waiting to take people downtown to see the fireworks. We had almost forgotten that it was the Fourth of July. We boarded a bus that was labelled Manhattan. It took a good two hours to get downtown as people were standing on the streets watching the fireworks. The bus finally stopped in the heart of the city, not far from 42nd Street where Cindy was roaming. By this time the fireworks were over.

It was hot, humid and dark with shoulder to shoulder people. It reminded me of the pictures we'd seen of the Boston Marathon. We were frustrated and miserable already. We saw a policeman standing close by, so we asked him where 42nd Street was. He pointed in a direction which turned out to be wrong, or else we were confused. We ended up at a seedy hotel that looked like a hang out for pimps and prostitutes. We were the only white guys there. We managed to find a phone to call home to see if Cindy had called and also to get the phone number of the private investigator, Tony.

The folks were glad to hear that we were there. There had been no news from Cindy, but Mom gave us the telephone number. We called the investigator and we were glad to hear that he had been expecting our call. Bob had clued him in, and he was willing to help. What a relief! It was aranged that he would come to the hotel and pick us up. We left the dingy hotel and sat down on the curb in front of it, two sorry looking misfits, waiting for Tony.

He pulled up about 10:00 p.m., and we climbed into his air-conditioned car with sighs of relief. He wanted more information. We told him that she had been at Covenant House on the previous day but that she had left for some reason. He suggested that we start by going to the Covenant House to inquire about Cindy. With the investigator giving us advice and taking us around, the situation didn't seem quite so hopeless. When we arrived at the Covenant House, we all got out of the car. We rang the doorbell and a man came out to talk to us. I noted that he shut the door behind him before asking us what we wanted. Tony explained that our sister was sick and had stayed there the night before; that we were her brothers, and we wanted to take her home. He showed his identification; we showed the picture of our family and our identification. We kept telling him that she was sick and needed to take lithium, but he stood there like a statue. He refused to say that she had been there, or that she was there, or that she had ever been there. Nothing. No amount of talk or proof that she was our sister made any difference to him. He had his orders. Finally, he told us to wait while he went inside. After a few minutes he came out and said, "All I can say is that she isn't here now." What a letdown!

Where to next? Cindy had told us that she had parked her car in a ramp near the Covenant House, so the three of us started searching the parking ramps. We talked to the attendants, showing them the photograph, but no one would say that they had seen her. We gave them a description of her car and the license number. We walked and walked from one large parking ramp to another, searching each floor. Nothing. By now we were so tired that had Cindy walked right up to us, I'm not sure we would have recognized her. The sea of faces had become a blur. It was midnight, and Tony suggested we get a room at the Ramada Inn on 42nd Street and start fresh in the morning. He dropped us off there, promising that he would be back to help us in the morning.

After we got to our room, we decided to talk to the parking attendant at the hotel as Cindy was supposed to have parked here as well. The attendant did not admit to having seen Cindy or the car. We went to our room and fell into bed exhausted. This was a Fourth of July that we could never ever forget!

Tuesday, July 5, 1983

The next morning we got up early with the same beaten feeling that we had the night before. We didn't take time for breakfast. We went immediately to the parking lot attendant at the hotel to find out if the day-shift attendant had seen Cindy or her car. We went through the same ritual of identifying ourselves and showing the photograph. He could hardly speak English, but his eyes lit up in recognition and, using a lot of gestures, he told us that he had seen her and her cat. We gathered that she had been there for a few days, but had paid the attendant and left. That information helped somewhat. We now knew she had told the truth about that at least.

We left the hotel and headed down to the place where she said she would be selling ice cream. When we found it, we had to wait for the guy to come to open up and get the ice cream carts out for business. It was about 9:00 a.m. when he came. Lon talked to him, giving him all the details. He emphasized the fact that Cindy was sick and that she needed help badly. He admitted that she had sold ice cream for him, but he was angry because he had bought her a cart, and she had not shown up for work on July 4th, the day he had needed her most. It became clear that this Egyptian vendor's cooperation could only be gained by offering money. He then told us that he knew where he could find her if she didn't come to work. We didn't trust him, but we knew that she had sold ice cream for him, and we thought that he might actually know how to find Cindy. Lonnie was dealing with him, so I don't remember the details except that he got one hundred dollars from us. Lonnie and I waited around until about 10:00 a.m., hoping that Cindy would turn up for work. While waiting, we talked to some parking lot attendants and others, showing the photograph and telling the same story over and over. There were some pretty decent guys here. They showed an interest and advised us where to look. I don't know exactly where we were, but it was near the Lincoln Tunnel, about six blocks from 42nd Street.

Around noon I took off alone to Macy's to check if Cindy could possibly be selling ice cream outside this store again. It was about a mile away, I think. The day was very hot and humid, and by the time I got to Macy's it had started to rain. It just poured buckets for about five minutes, and I was drenched. Then it stopped raining as suddenly as it had started, but the place still felt like a nauseating jungle with putrid odors of hot grease, food and garbage.

I didn't see Cindy, so I continued walking past Macy's, past the Empire State Building, hoping against hope that by some miracle I would see her. Now and again, I would see someone that looked like her, and I would run up to the girl only to be disappointed again and again. I continued on back to where Lonnie had been waiting for Cindy to show up for work. I got back to him about 2:00 p.m. or so.

For some reason, Tony hadn't come back to help us as planned, so we were on our own. We decided that, since Cindy hadn't shown up by now, she most likely wouldn't. Therefore, we might as well go back to 42nd Street. According to her phone calls, she had hung around mostly in the neighborhood of Blimpey's fast food restaurant.

When we got to 42nd Street, we kept displaying the photograph and asking if anyone had seen Cindy. Here, to our dismay, there was no cooperation at all. Lips were sealed, although twenty dollar bills helped a few to remember that maybe they had seen her around. However, at Blimpey's the manager came around the counter to take a look at the picture. "Why, yes, I have seen her. She sticks out like a sore thumb around here. Get her out of here before the pimps get her.

She has been here a lot!" He said this with such feeling that even though the news was good, we were more scared than ever that we might be too late. We just had to find her tonight. Right away, we renewed our desperate search with the awful feeling that we might be too late.

By now it was dark, but it was still hot and humid. Night people were selling their wares, sirens were blaring, lights were blinking, and marquees invited sex and violence. The dregs of humanity seemed to be everywhere; the stench was making me sick. How in the world could any young good-looking girl survive in such a hellish place? The frequent presence of police cars helped our spirits a little, but the thought of our precious sister walking these streets at night filled us with fear and the urgent need to find her NOW! We kept peering into faces, showing the photograph and inquiring.

Eventually, we decided that we had better call home to see if Cindy had called. When we got through to Mom she told us that Cindy had called earlier to say that she knew we were in New York looking for her; but, instead of saying that she would disappear as she had threatened, she said that she would meet us at the Ramada Inn next morning at 10:00. This was the best news that we had ever heard! I was so relieved that I felt weak and weepy and THANKFUL! "All the prayers," I thought, "that's what's doing it." Without the people at home praying, what chance would we have? Prayer had changed Cindy's mind. That had to be it. I felt so relieved and suddenly so hungry; but before eating, we called Tony to tell him the good news. He came to the hotel to visit with us that night and promised to come back next morning. We figured he could probably help us persuade Cindy to go back home with us but at that point in time, this seemed a rather small problem. We slept like two logs that night.

Wednesday, July 6, 1983

We got up this morning full of anticipation. It was about 9:30 a.m. when we went down to the lobby to wait for Cindy.

We didn't eat breakfast as we wanted to be close to the door, so that we'd be sure to see her. Ten o'clock came and went. No Cindy! Ten thirty came and went. No Cindy! We looked at each other with fear in our eyes and hearts. "She's not coming," I ventured. "Let's hit the streets," I suggested and Lonnie agreed. We went out into the heat, the wind knocked out of us. We were desperation and anxiety personified.

Lonnie took one side of the street; I took the other. After awhile, I got the worst stomachache. I tried to keep going, but I couldn't ignore it. I yelled to Lonnie that I had to go in for something to eat! He yelled back that we didn't have time to eat. I yelled back that I WAS GOING to get something to eat! I headed back to the Ramada Inn with Lonnie reluctantly trailing behind. God must have made us oblivious of all the cafes along the way because back to the Ramada Inn I went. WHY?! We walked into the cafe, had something to eat, got up to pay the bill. The cashier looked at us and said, "Is your name Nyflot?" Surprised, we both said, "Yes." She then told us that we had been paged awhile ago. We hurried to the phone to call home. Mom told us that Cindy had called to say that she would be late as she had overslept. Good news again! But now we were wary. Would she really come? Just then Tony walked in, and we told him what had happened. We were so glad that he was there as he gave us the support we needed. He waited with us. We were talking when Tony interrupted with, "There she is!" He recognized her first, although he had only seen her photograph. I had looked right at her but didn't recognize her. She didn't look like our well-groomed Cindy. She was wearing a wrinkled red-checked culotte outfit and sandals. She looked tired, drawn, thin and pale. It was obvious that she hadn't had much to eat or much sleep.

She just stood there, motionless. We hugged her and told her how happy we were to see her, but she stiffened. She was on the defensive. She immediately let us know that she had no intention of returning home with us. Next, she informed us that, at 11:00 a.m., she had an appointment with someone who was going to help her find a job. By then it was after eleven, and we all said we wanted to go with her. She agreed to let us come if we stayed far enough away. As we walked to the appointment, Tony asked Cindy some questions. He inquired about her education and job skills, and she told him that she had gone to college one year and business college. Tony said, "With skills like that, you can get a good job here. You can stay with me and my wife until you get settled. You can easily make $20,000." That really sounded good to her. Tony joked with her which helped to put her more at ease. We appreciated having Tony there. He was a life-saver.

When we got to Port Authority, we fell behind as Cindy had requested. She walked up to the man who had waited for her. He was black as coal. Tony recognized him as one of the numerous pimps. Cindy talked with him for a few minutes; then came back saying nothing. Being a waitress or whatever didn't seem so great to her after Tony's assuring her of a good paying job in a nice office.

Cindy told us that her suitcase was here and that she wanted to pick it up. That was fine with us. We followed her to the baggage department for lost luggage where Cindy walked up to the attendant and talked to him as if he were an old buddy. She then climbed under the counter saying to the attendant, "I'm going to get my suitcase." He responded, "Do you know where it is?" "Yah," she quipped, "I put it back here." They seemed to know each other quite well. Cindy must have talked him into letting her leave her stuff there for nothing. She didn't have any money. Like most hypomanics, she was friendly and talkative. Being good-looking made these aspects of her behavior even more engaging.

When we got back to the Ramada Inn, we left Tony, who assured us that we could call him again at any time. Now, we had to gain Cindy's confidence. We also had to keep her occupied as she was very restless and unstable. She was talking about saving New York from destruction, about the anti-Christ and about certain letters that had special meaning. She had racing thoughts, grandiose ideas and markedly impaired judgment — all symptoms of the manic phase of the disorder. We were so happy that she was with us, and we were determined not to let her out of our sight. What could we do to keep her busy and interested? I grabbed a brochure off the table in our room. City tours, that's it. We'll take a tour. Lonnie was not in the mood for a tour, but Cindy was hooked on the idea. I thought that as long as we were almost 2,000 miles from home with nothing else to do, we might as well see the sights now that we had our Cindy.

Cindy was starving, so we ate at the Ramada Inn first, and then walked to where the tickets were sold. On our way we passed a pizza vendor. Cindy wanted some pizza, so Lonnie had some with her. I couldn't eat any as everything smelled terrible to me. We bought the tickets and walked a few more blocks to board the tour bus. It felt so good to sit down in the bus with Cindy by my side. After awhile, the bus stopped by the Statue of Liberty and we got off to look around. There were more vendors around the Statue area, and Cindy, who was still hungry, had eyes only for vendors. I wanted to barf just looking at food, but Cindy ate two hot dogs with everything, and Lonnie ate one with her. From there we saw more sights including Greenwich Village, Grant's Tomb and St. Peters Cathedral. After awhile, Cindy fell asleep and slept until the tour was over. When she woke up, she was disgusted that she had slept through most of the tour.

On the way back to the hotel Cindy talked about where her car was parked, and also told us a little about Perez. She was worried about her little cat. We assured her that the cat was having a great time with his new found playmate.

Back at the hotel, Lonnie and I relaxed while Cindy took a shower and got into some clean clothes. When she was ready, she wondered what we were going to do. Lonnie and I were ready for sleep, but Cindy was full of energy. I suggested that we get tickets for the David Letterman Show. Cindy said that she had met someone in the park who would get us tickets. I knew that was just one of those "Follow me and I'll get you anything" types. I told her we would just go to the Rockefeller Plaza, where the show is taped, to see if we could get tickets.

It was early evening. It took us only a few minutes to walk from 42nd Street to Rockefeller Plaza, but the change was amazing — like going from night to day. A few steps from the ghetto, to all these corporate skyscrapers with men dressed in business suits doing million dollar transactions — it was like walking from hell to heaven.

At the Rockefeller Plaza we attempted to take the elevator up to the floor where they were taping, but the guards stopped us. Suddenly, everyone was running and people started yelling something about a celebrity. Cindy took off like greased lightning to see who it was. Everyone was running outside, but by the time we got there, the limousine had pulled out. We never did find out who was creating all the excitement. What should we do now? What else, but eat! Cindy wanted potatoes and gravy. We went to the fancy restaurant at the Plaza. It wasn't busy, so we were waited on right away. We could not order intelligently because the menu was written in French. We told the waiter that we wanted mashed potatoes and gravy in our order. He showed us something on the menu, but it meant nothing to us. We told him that as long as it included mashed potatoes and gravy, it would be fine. As we waited, we looked around the walls which were covered with pictures of celebrities. It certainly was a swank place. When the food came, we had a good laugh, the first one in ages. We had ordered hot beef sandwiches at $12 a plate. It tasted delicious; the best hot beef we had ever eaten.

After leaving the restaurant, we went out and sat down to relax in the Plaza. It felt so good to be sitting there with Cindy, just watching the people go by. It put a new light on everything. Here we were in the middle of New York, on a midsummer's evening, with our sister. Everything felt good right then. Cindy made the difference. She was sitting safe and momentarily content between her two brothers.

We reluctantly got up to head back to the hotel — nothing urgent now. We moseyed by another hot dog vendor. Believe it or not, Cindy thought she could eat another hot dog. We told her, "No, no, you can't!" But we ended up ordering her one. One bite was all she could take of it. During the two weeks she had been gone, she had lost a lot of weight but at this rate, we figured she would gain it back in two days!

Back at the hotel again, we casually broached the question of going back home. Cindy had been telling us that she would never consider returning home with us. Up until then we had just said, "Fine," to these assertions, but now we needed to get her to change her mind. She had to be persuaded to go back home with us. We told her that she just had to go home again — long enough to take care of things; then she could come back. We told her that we would pay for her ticket back. She wanted to believe us, but she was skeptical. We kept talking. "Cindy, your car is here — you're going to have to come back for your car," we argued reassuringly. We didn't care a hoot about her car, but that argument seemed to help convince her that she would be able to come back. In desperation, Lonnie told her that if we weren't telling her the truth, she could have his house. She made him put that in writing. In the same spirit of desperation, I promised her my Corvette if we were not telling the truth. I'm glad she didn't make me write THAT down! She was softening. We kept talking until she finally said, "Well, if I fly home with you, I'll have to fly back on the next flight." We both said, "Fine, fine." We called the airlines right away and made reservations for the first flight out, which was 10:00 the next morning.

As soon as that was settled, I went to bed and was out like a light. Not so for Lonnie. He was worried that during the night, Cindy might decide to leave. He had to do something to make sure that didn't happen. After Cindy went to sleep, he put a suitcase, an antiperspirant can, a shaving cream can and anything else he could find on top of the suitcase in front of the door. If she decided to leave, there would be noise — lots of it! During the night Lonnie woke up with a start! There was Cindy. "What are you doing?" Lonnie snapped. Cindy snapped back, "I'm going to the bathroom!" I was not aware of any of the goings on during that night.

Thursday, July 7, 1983

We got up the next morning eager to get to the airport. We took a taxi there without incident. We bought our tickets. Since there was a wait, we went to the cafeteria for breakfast. Lonnie and I were anxious to get on the plane. We were worried that Cindy might change her mind at the last minute. Finally, we were able to board the plane with Cindy reminding us, "I'm coming right back!" and our reassuring her with an emphatic, "Fine, Fine!" It seemed a long wait, but actually we were in the air in short order. Cindy talked herself to sleep and slept most of the way to Minneapolis. There we ate and watched Cindy, still worried that she might change her mind and take off. We got back on the plane together for the last trek to Grand Forks.

When we landed in Grand Forks, Cindy didn't want to get out. We told her that she had to, but she could go back to New York. We were the last ones off, and by then Mom was really bent out of shape. She was sure that Cindy had taken off. Cindy was reserved with the folks as she had been with Lonnie and me. They hugged her, but she acted as though they were strangers, not her parents.

When we got outside to the van, it wouldn't start. It took Lonnie about an hour or so to get it going. As we turned to go south to Fargo, Cindy asked why we weren't going home. We told her that we had to get some lithium from her doctor. Amazingly, this satisfied her. She was hungry for mashed potatoes and gravy again. When we got to Fargo, we stopped at Wendy's where she had to settle for a hamburger.

We arrived at the St. Luke's Hospital expecting everything to have been arranged, but the admission process seemed to take forever. When it was finally time to go up to the doctor, Cindy insisted that I go along with her and Mom. She was getting suspicious, and evidently felt that she could, for some reason, at least trust me. Anyway, Cindy, Mom and I went up to the psychiatric unit. We had to ring to get in, and Cindy was getting very uneasy about it all. Inside the lights were dim, and a few people were sitting around smoking. It looked very uninviting. Mom and I were ushered into a brightly lit room where we talked to a psychiatrist, an admitting nurse and a social worker. By now Cindy knew something was amiss. She had been left out in the lobby while Mom and I talked to these professionals. She knew she wasn't there just to get medicine, but she didn't panic yet.

She pulled out a pack of cigarettes and smoked one cigarette after another. Mom didn't know she smoked, and Cindy told her much later that smoking was the only way she could hurt Mom for what she was doing to her, so she did it with a vengeance. As we moved to the door to leave, Cindy walked with us. When she couldn't leave with us, she became hysterical, screaming that she hated all of us and that we had betrayed her! If I had felt bad before, it couldn't compare to the terrible gut-wrenching I was going through now. I knew we had to do what we had to do, but I could just feel the panic and desperation Cindy was going through, being left alone, locked up, when we had promised faithfully that she could go back to New York. "God take care of my precious sister. Make her happy and well again!" was my prayer.

The $5,000 cash that we had saved for necessities in the event that we would be forced to go bankrupt was not meant for that at all. If we had not had the cash on the Fourth of July to make the trip that day to find Cindy, I shudder to think of what might have become of her. It took exactly $5,000 to bring her home. "Thank you, God, for making it possible for us to go to New York, for making it possible for us to find her, and for leading us each step of the way."

Chapter 8

A MOTHER'S PERSPECTIVE

Sunday, July 3, 1983

Sunday afternoon Cindy called from the Covenant House to say that she now had a place to stay. I was so happy, but I wanted to talk to someone there to be sure that what she was saying was true. I told the person that I talked to that Cindy needed lithium, and she assured me that Cindy would be seen by a psychiatrist. What a flood of relief swept over me at these words! She not only had a safe place to stay until we could figure out what to do, but she would also be seen by a doctor! When Cindy got back on the phone, I told her that we could maybe send some money to tide her over.

Monday, July 4, 1983

The next morning I called to talk to Cindy. "She's not here anymore," I was told. "What do you mean, she's not there? I just talked to her from there," I objected, not believing what I was hearing. She went on to explain that she had broken the curfew rule and could no longer stay there. I felt weak. She was on the street again! New panic set in! I called her brothers right away, and asked if they would fly to New York to look for her. They were equally worried, and were willing to go right away. Without hesitation they agreed and within a few hours, they were on a plane to New York.

Tuesday, July 5, 1983

Tuesday evening the phone rang. When I lifted the receiver, I heard Cindy say, "The boys are here in New York looking for me, aren't they?" I didn't know what to say. She had said that if they did that, she would disappear, and we'd never see her again. I tried to deny it, but she retorted, "I KNOW they are here because some people have told me, BUT I'LL TALK TO THEM!" "Thank you, Lord!" I breathed. Cindy continued, "Tell them to meet me at the Ramada Inn at 42nd and 8th. I'll be there at ten." There are no words to express the feeling of relief, joy, and thanksgiving that enveloped me like a warm blanket.

Later, when the boys called home to find out whether or not we had heard from Cindy, I was able to give them the happy news that she would meet them next morning at ten. I knew their relief was as great as ours.

Wednesday, July 6, 1983

In the morning Jonathan and Indira, missionaries from India, came to visit and pray. They knew about Cindy, and we were happy to relate to them that the boys were meeting with Cindy at 10:00 that very morning. Just then, the phone rang. It was Cindy. She said she had overslept. Were the boys still there? She was on her way to the motel! "Oh, God, not this again! Please God!" I quickly told the others what Cindy said, and then dialed the Ramada Inn. The boys just had to be there. By then it was about 11 a.m. When we got through to the motel, they paged Lon and Jeff several times, but there was no answer. I hung up the phone, defeated. What do we do now? The Bible says that "the fervent prayer of a righteous man availeth much," and our guests prayed fervently for God's intervention in this situation. Oscar and I prayed through our tears. It seemed impossible to us, but "God specializes in things thought impossible." Jeff has told how God intervened and answered these prayers in a miraculous way.

Thursday, July 7, 1983

We had made arrangements with St. Luke's Hospital, so that we could take Cindy there as soon as she got off the plane. We drove to Grand Forks to wait for them. Jan and Carla were along.

When the plane landed, I was afraid that something dreadful had happened as they were the very last ones off. Finally, they came, Cindy walking slowly behind her brothers. I hugged her, but she didn't respond. She was stiff and formal at first. She had clearly lost weight and look bedraggled, but her behavior seemed okay so far.

When we got to the van, it wouldn't start; so we had to wait while Lonnie fixed it. Cindy then went into high gear, calling everyone, making arrangements, cancelling her apartment, and on and on. She was talking a mile a minute and showed virtually all the symptoms that I had read to her over the telephone.

My anxiety kept mounting as it seemed to be taking forever to get the van fixed. Finally, it started. It coughed and sputtered, but Lon managed to keep it going. When we turned south to go the Fargo, Cindy asked why we weren't going home. I told her that we were going to the hospital first. I had nagged her so much about taking lithium that she accepted my answer.

Taking her for in-patient psychiatric treatment was to be a recurrent nightmare.

Chapter 9

LOCKED UP!

(Cindy) Thursday, July 7, 1983

When I realized that the door of the hospital room was locked, I panicked. I screamed, "Let me out of here! You promised to let me go back to New York! I hate you. I HATE YOU!" I kept screaming at my Mom and my brother as they stood there helplessly. My family had betrayed me, and I vowed that I would have nothing to do with them again, ever!

I felt that I needed to be in New York to help people fight against the big corporations. That's where God wanted me to be! I believed this with all my heart, as far-out as it was. I was filled with rage against my family whom I had trusted. I hated doctors who claimed that I was mentally ill. The words "MENTALLY ILL' were written on some papers which they gave me to read. I circled these ugly words and vowed to myself that I would make them regret having said that I was mentally ill. I certainly was NOT mentally ill!

I managed to sleep a little during the night, and by morning I had calmed down dramatically. I knew there would be a court hearing, and I was confident that I would be released. I reasoned that they certainly could not lock up someone who was perfectly well in every way. When the doctor came in to see me in the morning, he made some remark about being glad to see me looking so good. I was as pleasant and charming as I could be to his face, but underneath I was seething. I asked when the hearing would be held. He told me he thought it would be Tuesday, July 12th. Five days to wait! It seemed like an eternity.

During those five days my Mom was with me most of the time, but I did my best to ignore her. Dad got the same treatment! When my brothers came to visit, I was openly hostile to those two traitors.

The days passed slowly by until my first hearing.

Tuesday, July 12, 1983

The day of the hearing finally came. Policemen arrived to escort me to the courthouse. At this point I was not so sick that I didn't feel somewhat humiliated.

I liked my defense attorney. I let him know that there was nothing wrong with me, and that I expected him to get me out of the hospital. I knew, however, that it was the judge who would determine my fate.

My mom testified against me. Jeff testified against me. My own family was against me. I hated them. They lied about everything! It was all untrue. One doctor testified against me, but his evidence was unconvincing. My attorney and the state's attorney presented their final arguments, but the judge could not make up his mind. He said that I was different from other manic-depressives who had appeared in his court. As far as he could tell I appeared to be well, and he ordered a further psychiatric evaluation.

In the evening another psychiatrist talked to Mom and me. After two hours or so, he told us that he could not recommend committal because, in his opinion, I was not a danger to myself or others at that time. Of course I was delighted with this opinion and could hardly wait for the hearing next day.

Wednesday, July 13, 1983

At the next hearing, the psychiatrist testified as promised in my favor. I did not have to be locked up, but the judge told me that I was court ordered to take lithium. I promised to take my lithium faithfully, and with that hollow promise I was free to go.

I now know that the court's decision was the worst thing that could have ever happened to me. I needed help so badly, and they let me leave.

I had no intention of taking any pills. In my mind I was not sick at all. I just can't believe that doctors, acquainted with the horrors of mental illness, would let this happen to me. Didn't they realize that roaming the streets of New York for days without money while spouting off to total strangers about saving the world from destruction was clearly indicative of mental illness? Wasn't walking among pimps, murderers and low lifes on 42nd Street hazardous behavior for a young girl? What does it take?

If my parents knew that I needed help, why didn't the professionals know? Had I been committed at this first hearing, I would have been spared so much suffering. The things that happened to me after I was released as I got more sick each day were much worse than what had happened to me in New York. I could have been spared all that, if only the professionals had acted professionally! Certainly they must have known that a mentally ill person whose judgment is seriously impaired cannot make a decision in her own best interest. The LAW that makes it possible for seriously mentally ill people to decide whether or not they should have treatment is PREPOSTEROUS! This law must have been made by people who were themselves mentally ill with impaired judgment. This law does not protect our human rights. My human right was to be well and for the professionals to do everything possible to help get me WELL! At this hearing I WAS DENIED THIS BASIC HUMAN RIGHT!

Chapter 10

A MOTHER'S PERSPECTIVE

Tuesday, July 12, 1983

A petition for committal had been filed at the local county court and a mental health hearing was scheduled for today. I thought that there would be no question that Cindy would be committed for treatment after all she had been through. I thought spending about a week on the streets of New York was evidence enough that her judgment was seriously impaired and that she was a danger to herself. How little I knew!

Cindy's psychiatrist witnessed in favor of commitment for in-patient treatment. He stated that while in the manic state it was possible to drop dead from exhaustion. This statement was challenged repeatedly. Cindy's attorney suggested that this was a gross exaggeration. He had never heard of such a thing. What Jeff and I told the court didn't seem to carry any weight at all.

The judge decided that he needed the opinion of another doctor before he could determine whether or not she required commitment. The testimony of this psychiatrist was not enough; consequently we were to tell our story over again to another doctor in the evening. I believed that surely a second opinion would find that she needed in-patient treatment. I stressed to the second doctor that Cindy was planning to go back to New York the minute she was released.

After two hours of evaluating Cindy's mental state, he told us that she was not a danger to herself or others at that time. He announced that he would testify to that effect next day if Cindy's condition was unchanged. He felt bad about my concern, but that was his finding. We had been going through hell these last months, but our concerns were not this doctor's concern, at least not now. Both Cindy and I liked him very much, but he let us down.

Wednesday, July 13, 1983

At the second hearing the doctor hadn't changed his mind. He felt that she could be treated as an out-patient. After hearing this, the judge ruled in favor of out-patient treatment.

Cindy promised the judge that she would take the lithium, but it was obvious that she did not regard herself as sick in any way and would not have taken a single tablet if I had not stayed with her!

Chapter 11

FREEDOM!

(Cindy) Wednesday, July 13, 1983

After the hearing, Dad, Mom and I went over to my efficiency apartment which was still waiting for me. Mom had been staying in the apartment while I was in the hospital, so the apartment was clean — not that I cared. Dirt and a mess didn't bother me anymore.

Mom insisted on staying with me. I didn't want her to for obvious reasons. I was free, and I wanted my independence. She wanted to stay to make sure that I took my precious pills and made it to the doctor's appointments. She was afraid I wouldn't take them, and she was right! I was not sick, and taking those pills would be evidence that I was manic-depressive or bipolar. And I was not!

At first I felt wonderful, so energetic, so happy. The fact that I slept very little and had to walk all the time and had no appetite to speak of was great as far as I was concerned. I would get up early, eat a little that was forced down my throat by my bothersome mother, then leave and roam all day and into the night.

The fact that Mom didn't see or hear from me all day and well into the night was no concern of mine. She could go home any time as far as I was concerned. I still wasn't sure whether I hated her or loved her.

I would take the pills when Mom gave them to me, but most of the time I just pretended to take them. I was spending much of my time walking in the parks. The leaves were so-o-o beautiful. I've learned since that this was due to heightened sensory perception in the manic state.

I walked from one end of Fargo and Moorhead to the other. The inner restlessness made it impossible to be quiet for long.

I would come back to the apartment in the wee hours of the morning sometimes, but Mom would always be waiting up for me with a hot dish or something for me to eat. I would be starved by then from all the walking. I did not have much money with me. Mom was worried that I would take off back to New York as I had threatened. I was always irritable and downright hostile when I returned to the apartment. I was unable to understand or appreciate anything my family was doing for me then. I just wanted them off my back.

Mom kept urging me to continue my secretarial course, and I did go back for a few days but I was getting much too sick for that. I went to the registrar to try to get my money back. I planned to use the money to go back to New York for my car. Wisely, they refused to give it to me. That made me angry, of course, so I had words with her which only reinforced the decision not to give the money to me. I walked out in a huff.

Thursday, July 14, 1983

I was walking on the sidewalk with this feeling of urgency which was with me all the time now. I had to do something about all the corruption in the world. I was obsessed by Orwell's book, "1984." It would soon be 1984, and I had to do something, so that all the evil prophesied would not come to pass. Hurry, hurry, hurry, there's so much to do, but with all the mixed up thoughts, no plan could ever be formulated.

Suddenly, I heard someone yell, "Hey, do you want a beer?" I looked around and saw two men sitting in a car beckoning me over. Of course I didn't hesitate a moment before rushing to the car. One said, "Get in." In I went. One man was blonde, nice looking, had a job, a car and seemed quite decent. The other was Mexican, ugly, an alcoholic without a redeeming feature that I can think of now as I look back. Who did I choose to be my special friend? The ugly Mexican! Why? Because I was sick, so sick, I was drawn to the sleazy, the sleazier the better. Because of my mixed up thinking, anyone who appeared decent was a part of the corrupt society. Good looked bad to me, and bad looked good. This Mexican was a creep of the worst kind. I could have been spared meeting this sleazeball, who took advantage of my vulnerability, if I had been forced to have treatment under lock and key after my first court hearing. I could have been spared so much suffering.

These two men roomed together in an older house. Now, on my walks, I would stop there. I couldn't stay long because of my restlessness, but I would stop there more and more often until it became a hangout for me.

Mom started coming to his house, trying to find me when it got late at night. Sometimes I would go home with her, but sometimes I would tell Peter to lie to her, and say that I wasn't there, or I'd gone to a bar. Sometimes Mom would bring the pills and beg me to take them even if I wouldn't come home with her. Once I remember spilling the whole bottle of pills on the ground in the dark.

Although my mother and I had always been so close, now in this state of mind I was unable to understand or feel any emotion except anger. What I was doing seemed perfectly normal to me then. A few months earlier I would never have been caught dead in a situation like this. Now I could not control my thoughts or actions. My whole life was out of control. I was driven, pushed and pulled from one direction to another by a force that made my life totally miserable eventually. This FORCE was the chemical imbalance in my brain. This was causing the messages to be garbled, to say the least. It was a biological problem, not a psychological problem, that was causing the bizarre behavior.

As the days and weeks went by I became more and more angry with the doctors and my family. I blamed them for all my misery. I couldn't understand what was happening to me. All I knew then was that I was miserable, and it was the doctors' fault. I became obsessed with the desire for revenge. I would sue the doctors!

Sunday, July 31, 1983

On this day I told my mother that she had to leave! I refused to come back to the apartment as long as she was there. I would not tolerate her crying and talking negatively to me. That was it! Once was enough!

The next day she left, and I threw my pills away. I was not sick and I didn't need the pills or the hassling!

Saturday, August 20, 1983

I managed somehow to get a waitress job, but it lasted for only one week. I was just too restless and confused to hold down a job. This Saturday, I was paid for my week of work. One of the busboys asked if I wanted a ride to get my check cashed. My car was still in New York, so I was glad to take him up on his offer.

After my check was cashed, he was taking me home when, out of the blue, he said, "Give me your money." I was shocked. "What are you saying?" I asked. "GIVE ME your money!" he repeated. I wasn't sure if he was joking or serious, but I wasn't about to take a chance. I opened the door and jumped out of the car while driving down University Avenue. Miraculously, I wasn't seriously hurt.

I was doing bizarre things like that more and more frequently. When I went to the lake with Peter and his friends, I would jump off the bridge into the racing water below. I had no idea that it was a dangerous thing to do.

I was becoming more and more irritable and restless. It was getting so bad that I could hardly stand it. My long walks weren't helping me feel much better now, and the hate I felt for the doctors was intensifying to the point that I felt that I had to do something about it. It was time for me to let my two former doctors know that I planned to sue them for millions. They were going to have to pay for making my life so miserable. It was all their fault!

Monday, August 22, 1983

This was the day that the doctors were going to learn about my wrath. I couldn't stand it any longer. I took my little recorder in hand, so I'd have our conversations recorded, just in case I needed it for the court hearings. I marched into the first doctor's office stating with all the fervor I could muster that I was going to sue him for a million dollars for saying that I had bipolar disease! It wasn't true. That was defamation of character. I then went to the second doctor's office and told him the same thing. Then I left, even before he could say a word. It made me feel a little better, I thought, knowing they were going to have to suffer also.

Tuesday, August 23, 1983

For some reason I was not out walking as usual. I was lying on the couch when I heard a loud knock on my door. When I opened the door, there stood a cop with my brother, Lonnie. I knew I had to get away from them. I didn't know how, but they weren't going to take me back to the hospital! The cop pulled out his handcuffs as he told me that we were going for a ride to jail.

Lonnie asked the cop not to handcuff me. He said that he would see to it that I wouldn't run away. Finally, the cop put the handcuffs away, and they walked on each side of me.

When we got outside, I broke away and ran. Of course, my long-legged brother caught me. I kicked and screamed, bringing people out on their balconies. The cop put me in handcuffs as the people were yelling obscenities at the cop and my brother for treating me like that. I HATED my brother for this. I had no idea what agony he was going through having to be part of this nightmarish scenario. I was hauled to the police station to wait for my court hearing. This was my second trip to jail in handcuffs.

Thursday, August 25, 1983

The day of my court hearing arrived. I was brought to court from jail by another policeman. After hearing the testimony of the doctors, my family and the lawyers, I knew they had all conspired against me.

Now my third doctor who had witnessed that I was not a danger to myself at the last hearing, reversed his testimony, saying that I should be treated as an in-patient. My own lawyer turned against me too. His recommendation was that I be placed in the hospital for two weeks for further evaluation. How could he? He was supposed to be on my side. I was perfectly well and even my own lawyer turned against me. I fired him on the spot!

My mom testified at every hearing, and she was against me every time. I was alone and desperate.

Chapter 12

A MOTHER'S PERSPECTIVE

Wednesday, July 13, 1983

After Cindy was released for out-patient treatment, I stayed with her at the apartment in Fargo. However, she was seldom in the apartment. She was forever out walking. She would walk all over the city and come back late in the evening still restless but also hungry, unreasonable, irritable and miserable. Her judgment was becoming more and more impaired. Her usual inhibitions were almost gone. The friends she chose were unsavory and there wasn't a thing I could do but see that she took the pills, take her to her doctor's appointments, be there for her and PRAY. I prayed for her protection until the lithium would stabilize her moods. I trusted God to answer that prayer. If I hadn't done that, I would have not been able to stand the stress and heartache. My quiet, shy daughter, who had a special talent as a classical pianist, was gone.

After about three weeks she seemed a little better. She told me one morning, "I guess you didn't have any choice but to come and take me back from New York. I sure don't feel high today, but I don't feel depressed either. Maybe this is the way I'm supposed to feel." However, the next weekend she insisted that I go home.

Sunday, July 31, 1983

What precipitated Cindy's determination that I leave was an unfortunate, disastrous happening. It was a beautiful Sunday afternoon. My sister and her daughter had just gone back to Minnapolis after a miserable visit with Cindy and me. I made the mistake of suggesting to Cindy that we go to Detroit

Lakes, Minnesota, to relax on the beach. She never spent any time with me in the apartment, and I thought that this would be a pleasant way to spend an afternoon together, instead of my pacing the floor waiting, worrying and wondering where and how she was. How foolish of me!

Surprisingly, Cindy was eager to go. She had been attending business college again and was behind in her school work, of course; so she took her books along to get caught up. That was her idea.

On the way to the lake she revealed that some of her "friends" were tubing down a river about five miles from the lake. A red alarm went off in my head! On, no! When we got to the beach, she did start on her schoolwork. She wanted help with her English assignment. However, the assignment was punctuation, and she did each sentence so fast that I could not keep up. I couldn't believe how fast she was doing it, and it was all done correctly. If she asked a question, she would not wait for the answer. She went through six pages so fast that my head was spinning. Then she told me that she was going to do her math and needed a calculator from the car, but said, "Don't come with me, I'll be right back." After all we had gone through, I still trusted her word! When she didn't come back after 15 or 20 minutes, I rushed to the place the car had been parked. There was no car! Cindy had taken it. "Oh, God! What can I do now?" I threw her quilt on the ground and sat down on it to cry in desperation, first because of my concern for her, but also for being such a fool. I couldn't seem to get it through my head that a person with this illness cannot be trusted when in a high or manic state. They will do things which they would never, never do when well!

I knew she must have gone tubing on the river, but I had no idea when or if she would come back. I waited for awhile and was becoming more and more upset, so I decided that I just had to call someone. I finally got through to Lonnie's wife, but Lonnie was sick with one of his terrible migraine headaches, and the company they had invited was just arriving. As I hung up the phone, Cindy drove by. Thank God!

I knew very well that crying in front of Cindy was taboo as this only caused her to become frustrated and angry. Up to this point I had been able to keep my emotions in check in her presence, but now I was too far gone after so many weeks of stress. All it took for the floodgates to open was Cindy yelling out the window as she drove by, "Where's my quilt?" One of her quilts had been stolen in New York, and she didn't want this one lost. I knew that, but yelled back, no doubt with my face all blotchy and contorted, "I don't know and how could you do this?" As soon as I used that tone of voice, she became hostile. I got in on the driver's side and turned into a driveway in order to head the car for home, crying the whole time. She yelled, "I'm getting out of here!" She proceeded to open the car door to get out. I grabbed her swimsuit, a one piece, and hung on for dear life. If she left, I didn't know what she would do. I could hardly breathe. She screamed, "You're crazy!"

By this time people had gathered around, cars were honking as we were backed halfway onto the road, so I was forced to let go, and she was gone. This was my punishment for allowing myself to let go and cry. As I pulled out, a policeman yelled, "What's going on here?" I was still crying and told him that my daughter had bipolar disorder and had run away. He would have understood the situation better perhaps if I had said she was mentally ill.

Eventually the police found her, and I saw her in the passing police car. By the time I got to the police station, she had them all convinced that I was crazy, and my appearance certainly tended to confirm her story. She had persuaded them that she, rather than I, should drive as I could not be trusted behind a wheel. I didn't want to contradict her and cause more of a fuss, so I acquiesced. What a drive that was! I learned what the expression, "Drives like a maniac," meant.

By some miracle, we did get to the river. She jumped out of the car and insisted that I meet her "friends." She had changed from near hysteria to total calm in the second it took to get out of the car. I managed to greet her friends and then drove back to Fargo totally drained. If only I hadn't lost control. She did not come home with me, nor did she come home that night.

She called late that evening to tell me that she would not come back to the apartment as long as I was there. She wanted me to leave and that was that.

Monday, August 1, 1983

Monday morning Cindy went to see the judge to give her version of the incident. Apparently, he believed every word and told her that her mother was entirely too domineering, and that it would be good for her to get away. Cindy asked him if she could leave Fargo. He said she could, if she came to him first to let him know. No one, even yet, could really tell that Cindy was ill.

After her talk with the judge, she came back to the apartment. When she found me still there, she became upset and insisted that I had to go. She would not come back to the apartment as long as I was there. I had no choice.

Cindy walked with me to the door and stood there as I walked down the hall. When I turned to tell her that I loved her and would be calling, the expression on her face broke my heart. It said to me, "Mom, I love you. I don't know why I'm doing this!" I turned quickly and rushed out, not wanting her to see the tears or hear the sobs.

Before leaving town, I tried to talk to her psychiatrist, but he was not available. However, I did manage to speak with her counselor. He told me in a dry, matter-of-fact way that Cindy might never get well if she continued to refuse to take her medication. His attitude seemed to be a nonchalant, "That's the way the cookie crumbles." He told me that I'd better come to grips with that! Some comfort and encouragement he dished out! My tears were a puzzlement to him. I left his office feeling much worse, if that were possible, than when I entered. I managed to keep myself under control until I got into the car. Then I howled and cried all 150 miles home. I had to have the window open as the air conditioner wasn't working, so I'm sure my wailing was heard and was a puzzle to many as I drove through towns and passed cars.

Cindy had always been threatening to go back to New York for her car, and now that I wasn't with her I was sure that she would follow through. I called her every day to make sure she hadn't gone. Sometimes I wouldn't find her at home until the middle of the night.

Then the time came that I called and called, all day and night, but no answer. I was positive that she had taken off for New York. I knew that she had an appointment with this "magnanimous" counselor of hers, so in desperation I called him. I asked if Cindy had come to her counselling session. He flatly refused to tell me anything, stating that the Privacy Act forbade him. I pleaded, "Can't you tell a mother who is worried sick that she has left for New York?" I need to know if she is still in Fargo." He replied in his unemotional, unconcerned tone, "No, I can't." How anyone could be so unfeeling and heartless is beyond me.

What was he doing in this profession? He should have been working in a quarry with stones, not with people! If he had been the least bit sensitive, he would not have responded as he did, in spite of the Privacy Act. Insensitive clods are obeying the letter of the law, rather than the spirit of the law. How comforting it would have been for us if he had just said, "Yes, she was here." We learned later that she had been to her session. Who would sue him for that?

This counselor as well as other professionals told me that it was Cindy's right to choose not to take medication, and it was her right not to be committed, and it was her right to be sick. I argued that she was sick and miserable, and that it was her right to have the chance to get well when help was available. At one point, I wrote to our state's attorney saying, "Cindy is not rebelling against God or her parents. She is sick and there is not a thing we can do to help her!" On another occasion I wrote to him again saying, "I am a director of a DAC for mentally handicapped adults, and our purpose is to get people out of the institutions and into the community where they can live as normal lives as possible. However, in cases such as Cindy's where there is such dramatic help in such a relatively short period of time, after which they can live normal lives, treatment is the only thing to do! Cindy wants to be well, but her impaired judgment and frustration make her unwilling to take the medicine. She told us today that she has been going through hell ever since she left for New York, and she wonders why God is allowing her to suffer so much."

After I left Cindy's apartment, Cindy quit taking lithium, quit business college and found a job as a waitress. She had all her clothes packed for her trip back to New York. Later, she made plans to move out of her apartment into another one. As the illness became progressively worse, the quality of life became as bad as it could be. This had to change! There was help for her illness, and we, her family, were going to do whatever we had to do to get the help she needed so desperately!

Thursday, August 25, 1983

At the hearing following her arrest, Cindy's doctor recommended in-patient treatment. However, in cross examination, when asked if she couldn't stay with her parents, he reversed his testimony and said that it might be an alternative to commitment. I was scared to death that the judge would go along with this alternative. Cindy's lawyer, however, recommended that she be committed for two weeks for observation. He obviously knew she was ill, and that if she wouldn't stay in Fargo, she certainly would not stay with her parents.

Afterward, when we thanked him for his understanding, he told us that if she were his daughter, he would want her to be given treatment involuntarily, if necessary. We were so grateful to him. This lawyer had never before recommended this, so the judge ruled that she be committed for two weeks. Cindy promptly fired her lawyer as she still did not realize that she was sick.

Since we did not have hospital insurance at this time, she could not be re-admitted to St. Luke's. Instead, she was taken to the state hospital a 100 miles away.

During this evaluation, she would not be forced to take lithium. She would have to take it voluntarily or not at all.

Friday, August 26, 1983

The morning after the hearing Oscar and I drove to Jamestown to see Cindy. We drove slowly up the hill on top of which sprawled the state hospital. Although it was a sunny morning, there was a heaviness in my chest.

We climbed the steps to RT 2, the unit which was kept locked. Here our precious daughter would be spending the next two weeks, at least. We rang the bell and were allowed to enter. A few of the patients came over to talk to us. One asked who we had come to visit.

When we said that Cindy was our daughter, he said, "Oh, we think she's beautiful!" The others agreed. I said, "Thank you. We think so too." That pleasant greeting from these hurting people lifted my spirits a trifle.

By now Cindy had been told of our visit, and she came out from her room. An attendant ushered us into a small visiting room.

I had been getting more upset each day at her refusal to take her pills, so when we got into the little room, I asked Cindy once again if she wouldn't take the lithium. Her answer was, "Why should I take medicine when I'm not sick?!" In my desperation I threw my thyroid pills on the floor, so that they went rolling in every direction, saying, "I will not take another pill until you do!" Cindy got right down on her knees, picking up the pills, and was so concerned that I take MY medicine.

When she had them picked up, she thrust them in my lap. Then she rushed out to tell the nurse on duty how unreasonable I was. I NEEDED medication and was refusing to take it just because I thought that she needed lithium. Her thinking was so impaired at this point that she couldn't be reached by this dramatic action either. She did NOT take the lithium offered her during these two weeks. Instead she hid them in her purse.

Her next hearing was scheduled for Friday, September 2nd, but due to the judge's illness it was canceled. It was re-scheduled for September 8th, but the psychiatrist got sick. It was re-scheduled for September 9th, but it was canceled again. Finally, on Wednesday, September 14th, the hearing took place. Those cancellations were a time of immense stress for all of us, but especially for Cindy. She had been counting the days, and this was two whole extra weeks to wait.

Chapter 13

THE INSTITUTION!

Thursday, August 25, 1983

After the hearing, at which I was condemned to two weeks in a psychiatric ward, all I could think of was my hate for everyone who had done this to me. Later, the drumbeat in my head became, "I have to get out of here! I have to get out of here!" This overwhelming desire dictated my every thought and action.

Handcuffed to a policeman, I was ushered into RT2. When the door slammed shut, I knew I was locked in. I ALSO knew that somehow I was going to escape from this awful place.

I paced the halls. Then I started writing feverishly, thinking that I was writing profound truths. I had so many important things to say to the world. I filled notebook after notebook with these words of great wisdom that I was given. Actually, it was all garbage!

Friday, August 26, 1983

The morning after my arrival, my folks came to see me. I felt betrayed by them, so I was angry and hostile. Mom kept bugging me about taking lithium, but I was not about to admit that I needed it. No way. Mom then did an incredibly stupid thing; she threw her thyroid pills on the floor, and said she would not take her pills until I took mine. I rushed out to tell a nurse what my mother had done and how unreasonable she was. This, I thought, would shame my mother and put a stop to that nonsense. I felt this nurse was more of a friend to me than my parents. This twisted thinking persisted.

Sunday, August 28, 1983

A preacher came to see me. He was very nice, but he didn't understand much about mental illness. While he was talking to me, I took the Bible, and threw it on the floor. He thought that was an act of rebellion against God, so he lectured me about that. The fact was that I loved God and that fact had not changed no matter how sick I got. Things I did while sick made little or no sense. When I drank, smoked and sinned in so many ways, I was not aware that it was wrong. I did not know right from wrong. That may be hard to believe, but it is true nevertheless. I never wanted to do anything that would displease God.

This pastor thought that I needed the Lord. I did, but not in the way he meant. I had been brought up in a Christian home and had committed my life to the Lord. This had not changed. I could not be responsible for the things I did and said while I was so sick.

Throwing the Bible on the floor was just the beginning of a series of acts that made it abundantly clear that I was not thinking or acting rationally. I called New York all the time, especially Lawyer Jim. I needed his advice for the hearings and how to get out of there. I even called the White House at one point. I don't remember what great pearl of wisdom I was going to tell them, but I didn't get through to the president. I called home several times a day except on weekends when Mom was with me.

Tuesday, August 30, 1983

My first really big plan was to incite a riot. I talked to almost all of the patients asking them to go along with my plan. The plan was that at noon this day we were all going to throw our trays of food on the floor. Each person I talked to said he would do it. I told them to throw their trays when I yelled,

"Now!" Everyone seemed enthusiastic about the idea. This was going to be fun! I went around reminding them of what we were going to do. I called home to tell Mom of my great plan. I'm sure that made her day!

Finally, it was noon and the trays were sent up. When everyone had received a tray, I yelled, "Now!" and threw my tray on the floor with a loud crash. But, lo and behold, my tray was the only one on the floor! What happened? I looked around, and everyone was eating their food; some sheepishly, I imagined. I should have been terribly embarrassed because I ended up having to clean up the mess and go without food and, I must add, they had delicious food. My riot was a fizzle, but I was undaunted.

Thursday, September 1, 1983

I had to get out of this place. A wide hall extended from one end of the unit to the other, and I was pacing a path, back and forth. Others paced with me, or alone. It was becoming more confining and suffocating by the day. At one end of the hall was the men's section; at the other end was the women's. In the men's section, there was a small visiting room which was opened only for visitors. In the women's area there was a small lounge with a stereo, radio and television. Between the sections there was a common area with tables where we ate our meals or mingled. There were about 20 of us in this particular place. There were two rooms that I called torture chambers; one for the men and one for the women. Now I can understand the need to place an extremely manic patient in a room away from all the stimuli of lights and activity which might make him worse, but I was always put in this isolation room as a punishment, as were others.

The doors to our rooms were locked part of the time because some who were depressed wanted to sleep all the time. So we were locked in from the outside world, and we were locked out of our rooms. The telephone was the only contact

I had with the world outside! It hung on the wall of the women's isolation room, across from the desk. I called many times every day.

I had a new plan! I went to the phone and called Jim, one of my "friends." I asked him to bring me a wire cutter. I don't think I told him why I wanted the wire cutter because I was afraid someone might overhear. He drove the 100 miles from Fargo almost right away, but he wasn't allowed to visit me because he had been drinking. I called him that evening to find out why he hadn't come, so he filled me in. He assured me that he would be there on the following afternoon.

As usual, I couldn't sleep but consoled myself with the thought that I would be out of this dreadful place next day. My plan would work. I just knew it.

Friday, September 2, 1983

I could hardly wait for Jim to come. Right after noon lunch he came. I asked an attendant to open the door of the little visiting room. As soon as the door was shut, I asked in a hoarse whisper, "Do you have the wire cutter?" "Sure do!" he said as he took it out of his pocket. I grabbed it from him and stuck it in my jeans out of sight. 'What are you going to do?" he whispered. Then in a hushed, but excited voice, I told him. "The bathroom windows have metal mesh across them. I'm going to cut the mesh, open the window and jump out. It's only about a 15 foot drop to the ground below. I will be out of here by dark!" He must have been as naive and dumb as I was because he did not question the wisdom of the plan. All he said was, "Do you want me to wait for you down by the highway?" I hadn't thought that far ahead, but I readily accepted his offer. I couldn't wait to get going on my escape plan, so I ended the visit by getting up and saying, "You'd better go now."

As soon as he left, I hurried to the bathroom and started cutting the wires. Janna, my special friend, came into the bathroom. I told her what I was doing, and asked if she wanted to come with me. "Yes, I sure do. I'll help!" She was pregnant, but a 15 foot jump didn't phase me. I told her to watch the door for snoopy nurses. I cut and cut the wire while, with a warning from me not to snitch, patients came in and went out. Finally, all the mesh was cut and, with a big sigh of relief, I pushed open the window. It would be a piece of cake, but the window needed to be opened wider so that I could crawl out. I pushed and pushed, but it wouldn't budge. I asked Janna to help, but to no avail. I could not get my body squeezed through the small opening. All of a sudden two attendants came bursting into the room yelling, "What's going on here? Cindy, get out of there this instant! Look at those wires! They're cut!" They started looking for the cutter, which I had stuck in my jeans. All the staff searched frantically and eventually concluded that I must have them. One of the attendants told me to put my pajamas on, but I refused. I told them that I would put my pajamas on if they left. There were male nurses and attendants as well as female. I despised these authority figures. They fought with me, pulling my clothes off until they found the cutter. Even after they had found the wire cutter, they kept hassling me. They dragged me away from the others to another floor and threw me into another seclusion room.

There was a mattress on the floor, but that was all. I put this mattress up on end in front of the window. I wanted them to have to open the door to check. I'd hear them say, "Is she in there? Did she get out somehow? She's hiding." Then they would open the door, and I would fight to get out. I couldn't stand being locked in an even smaller space than the unit itself. They tied my legs together. When they left, I worked until I got my legs untied. That's the way I was treated when I was sick.

Ostensibly, seclusion was used to calm a hyperactive or manic patient, and it was sometimes used for that purpose. But in actuality, it was primarily used to punish us for things we did; things we did as a result of our illness. The isolation room had a paradoxical effect on me. I panicked and hyperventilated. When I asked when I would be getting out, they ignored me or told me nothing. That was torture in itself — not knowing how long I would be forced to stay in that stark, stifling room. I was there all night.

Saturday, September 3, 1983

The next morning I was allowed to return to the others in the unit. When I went to the bathroom, I saw that the window had been boarded up. I thought to myself, "Wood! Ha! I can take care of that. They're not going to keep me here. No way. I know what I can do about that!" Even though the night before I had not been able to get the window open enough to squeeze out, I still was sure I could get out of that window. I sneaked in with deodorant spray and a deodorant stick which I smeared on the wood, thinking that would act like kerosene to help it burn when I torched it. My torch was my cigarette lighter. I kept trying to get the wood burning. While I was doing this, a little lady shuffled into the bathroom and went into the stall without a look or even a word although the smoke was rather thick. On her way out I told her to keep her mouth shut. She shuffled back out, and I was left to make my great escape.

The smoke was getting so bad that it was escaping under the door and into the hall. I just stood there, not realizing there was any danger. Again, the door flew open and a male attendant rushed into the smoke-filled room. "What the hell is going on here?" he cried. I ran out of the bathroom and hid in a cupboard. The seclusion room! How I dreaded the seclusion room. I knew that I was doomed now.

Eventually they found me, of course. This time it was worse than my wire cutting escapade. I was not only endangering myself, but others as well. There was the same fight as the night before. They found the lighter but only after a struggle with screaming and kicking. The seclusion room was too good for me this time! They tied my hands and feet to the bed, so I couldn't move. The bed was placed in the hall for everyone to walk by and gawk. As I recall the scene now, I am mortified but, at the time, all I could think of was getting out of there, and no amount of punishment could change that. I could not control my thoughts and actions. I was to be tied to the bed until the next morning.

Even though I may not have understood everything, it would have been so nice if the nurses and attendants would have talked to me and explained what was happening. I wanted to be treated like a human being with feelings even though I was giving them a bad time. I would never have acted like that if I hadn't been sick. Letting me know that they understood that I was not responsible for what I was doing, would have helped me get through those days and weeks. My court hearing had been canceled, and I had been counting the days until my hearing. No one seemed to understand or care what I was going through. There is a need for more compassionate people working with the mentally ill. I now know that I was very rebellious and belligerent. I tried their patience, but an explanation of the things that were happening to me would have been comforting. I wanted to do good and at the same time I was doing everything bad. This was just the opposite of what I wanted to do. At the time I could not discern right from wrong, dangerous from safe or rational from irrational. My inhibitions were gone. I was not the modest, shy girl that I had always been. These escapades took place during the first two weeks while I was being evaluated. By all these antics, I had really pounded the nails in my coffin securely. Had I only known! My next hearing was set for Thursday, September 8. I had circled that important day and was checking off each day until this, my fourth hearing, would take place.

Thursday, September 8, 1983

I was so happy when this day arrived. However, my happiness was to be short-lived because I soon learned that my hearing had been canceled again. Someone else was sick.

No one knows how awful I felt when I heard that. I was sure that I would be released at my next hearing, and this meant that I would be incarcerated longer. Even a day was too long, but the hearing was re-scheduled for the next day.

Friday, September 9, 1983
The hearing was canceled again! No one cared how I was suffering by all these cancellations; at least I never heard anyone say they felt bad that I had to wait for a third time. Mom had not been notified of the cancellation, so she came from Fargo to visit me. She was with me weekends. I was beginning to look forward to her coming because it helped to break up the sameness of each day. Also, it was such a relief to be able to go into the visiting room, a welcome change of scenery from the rest of the unit. I wanted to spend almost all the hours with my mom in this little room. I felt privileged to be apart from the others in this special room. It contained a table, a couch, a lounging chair and two straght chairs, that was it. But I liked it!

Wednesday, September 14, 1983
Finally, the hearing was to take place. I was up early as we were leaving for Fargo at 8:00 a.m. The hearing was at 10 a.m. Once again I was taken by a policeman to jail to await the hearing.

When I was brought into the courtroom, my new lawyer was there to defend me. I had talked to him on the phone many times.

I looked around the room, and I saw many of the staff from the institution present. What were they doing here? Mom was sitting in the third row as usual. I expected that she would testify against me as usual. However, this was one time that she did not have to say a word. The staff said it all. They had the wire cutter there in evidence as they related that story. They had the cigarette lighter there in evidence as they related the other story. They testified that I had not taken a single lithium tablet. When it was all over, I was sentenced to another 30 to 90 days in that horrible place. This was one of the worst days of my life. I felt totally devastated. How was I going to be able to live 30 more days in that place? I would just have to escape. That was all there was to it.

Now, of course, I am glad for that verdict, but at the time I was full of hate for everyone who had done this to me. I cried and would not be comforted by my mother. She was against me too.

I was taken back to jail to wait until the police could take me back to the state hospital at Jamestown. Mom followed behind in her car. She was always there.

When we got back and walked into RT2, it seemed that I was going to spend the rest of my life in that wretched place. The patients rushed over to me to ask what had happened, but I didn't want to talk. I was desperate, and life was not worth living! Everyone was against me: my family, my doctor, the staff, everyone! I didn't have a friend in the world. Oh, yes, I had ONE friend!

I hurried to the phone and called this "friend," Lawyer Jim! I asked him what I should do, and he advised me to appeal the decision. After I hung up the phone, I called my new lawyer about this, but he gave me some excuse for not doing that. There was no one to help me. I was alone and life had no meaning.

I was now compelled to take lithium medication, but I persistently fooled the staff into believing that I was taking it when, in reality, I was hiding the tablets. After two weeks of this my doctor became suspicious because my lithium level didn't change. Then they started giving me lithium in liquid form instead of tablets. I was hard pressed to know how to avoid swallowing that. It tasted terrible but down it went. They watched to see that I did not spit it out. I started writing again. I composed a couple of songs. Earlier, I had traded my flute for a small lap organ. I used this for my composing, such as it was. It was not great, but it kept me occupied.

I was still telephoning everyone I knew, and everyone I didn't know. I was calling those New York numbers that I had collected on the streets. I often called a guy with whom I thought that I was madly in love. He was one of my obsessions. I told him that I was in an institution and that he had put me there, and then laughed to let him know that I was just kidding.

I repeatedly tried to escape and consequently was put in the seclusion room. Sometimes it was for 15 minutes, sometimes for an hour or much longer. When others were put into the seclusion room, I would feel sorry for them, and I would push a cigarette under the door and talk to them. This was against the rules, so I would be put into seclusion next.

Mom came on Friday evenings and stayed until Sunday afternoon. We did a lot of walking in the halls and sitting in the visiting room where I would do all the talking. I still thought that I hated her, but I would have my head in her lap and be holding her hand most of the time, even when I was reaming her out about some imagined injustice.

After I was forced to take lithium in liquid form and the antipsychotic medication, thiothixene (Navane), I started getting better. This earned me the privilege of going downstairs to eat a meal. We walked down in a line like jailbirds. As we walked past a door, I couldn't resist trying the handle, and it OPENED! Once again I was off like greased lightning. Of course I was caught and put in the stabilization room as the seclusion room was sometimes called. I spent hours in there that time, but no amount of punishment changed my behavior. I could not control my actions as those in charge seemed to believe was possible. I feared this room more than I can express, yet time and time again I disobeyed the rules and ended up being shoved into that hellish room.

A few days later I had earned another privilege. I could go to the pool room. While there, I asked if I could go to the bathroom, and the supervisor said, "Go ahead, that's fine."

As I walked down the hall there seemed to be no one around, so again I could not resist the temptation of trying to escape. I ran down the hall, out the door and into the yard.

One of the patients, with whom I had had a hair-pulling fight, saw me and squealed, "I'm going to tell on you." She disappeared into the building and did her dastardly deed. I ran toward the freeway, hoping to hail down a car. I was caught before I got that far. Now I had to face that seclusion room again.

When we got back to RT2, I dashed to the phone and managed to get through to Mom. I screamed into the phone, "Mom, they are going to put me into the seclusion room again! Please, mom do something! Don't let them put me in the seclusion room again!" The attendants were trying to shut me up, and they finally dragged me away with the phone dangling and with Mom hearing me scream as I was forced into the room to be punished once again.

While I was in the institution, I thought that the people who were there with me were as well as I thought I was. Now that I have been back there to visit, I realize how very sick we all were. I'm so thankful for the medicine that has worked so well for me, but my heart goes out to those who are still there. I just wish there was something more that could be done for them. I pray that through research more and better cures will be found to help everyone who suffers from this terrible illness.

Saturday, October 1, 1983

After taking all the medication given to me for two weeks, I was getting better. This Saturday when Mom was visiting, I took out my little tape rcorder and taped our conversation which was as follows:

Cindy: (Sarcastically) "In Jamestown Hospital just having a really good time, I tell ya, with my mother LaVerne. So do you have anything to say to the recorder? Say, "Hi, Cindy is bipolar."

LaVerne: "O.K. Cindy is bipolar."

Cindy: "Cindy is NOT bipolar. Mother thinks I am bipolar. I think I'm not bipolar. Lonnie thinks I'm bipolar. Jan, Carla. Um-m Dad, Mom, doctors. A, B, C, D, the judge, but yet I don't think I'm bipolar, and I'm going to prove it somehow. We're sitting in Jamestown State Hospital right now, and I'm going to have a little interview with my mother. Well, mother, I've been in here for 38 days, and do you feel there has been a great change in my personality since that first day that you committed me to St. Luke's Hospital in Fargo, July 7, 1983?"

LaVerne: "Yes, there's a big difference."

Cindy: "Now would you explain this great difference in me? First of all, tell me how I was acting before I went into the hospital."

LaVerne: "Well, you went to New York and . . . (Cindy interrupting)

Cindy: "What's wrong with going to New York, a young girl wanting some excitement out of life and wanting to get a waitress job in New York city. What's wrong with that?"

LaVerne: "Ending up on the streets without any money in a very dangerous big city . . . (Cindy interrupting)

Cindy: "But Cindy did not end up on the streets. She ended up in the Covenant House, and she had a place to rest her head in a comfortable bed every single night."

LaVerne: "On the floor."

Cindy: (interrupting) "Not on the floor! Mother was not there. She doesn't know where I slept each night. Mother, do you feel there were pimps trying to get hold of me while I was in New York?"

LaVerne: "Most certainly."

Cindy: "I say there were no pimps trying to get me because not one of them tried to hurt me in any way whatsoever, and I took no offers. They're very wise, you know. They just can't take you, pull you off the streets, Do you feel that Lawyer Jim is a pimp?"

LaVerne: (wary) "You want me to . . . You want that to be on tape so that you can send it to him and that he'll sue us? Is that what you are trying to do?"

Cindy: "She thinks I'm going to sue when I'm going to erase this because it's just a little bit of a joke here. Do you feel that the other black guy that I came across was a pimp?"

LaVerne: "Yah, I think there were a lot of pimps that were after you.."

Cindy: "Do you feel that I did not take care of myself adequately?"

LaVerne: "Yes . . ."

Cindy: (interrupting) "Which I did. I took a shower every day. Do you feel that I didn't get enough food to eat?"

LaVerne: "Yes . . ."

Cindy: (interrupting) "I had places to eat every day. U-m-m-m, do you feel that I was in a manic state while I was in New York?"

LaVerne: "You were in a manic high."

Cindy: "Do you feel that I'll ever get into a depressed situation again?"

LaVerne: "Not if you take your lithium."

Cindy: "Why is lithium so important for me to take?"

LaVerne: "Because it will normalize your chemical imbalance."

Cindy: "Why? There's no proof that I have a chemical imbalance. That doesn't show up on the tests, so how can you be absolutely sure that I have a chemical imbalance?"

LaVerne: "Because the doctors know, and you had .03 lithium level. Now we'll see what it is on Monday."

Cindy: "Do you respect Dr. A?"

LaVerne: "Yah, I think so. Yes."

Cindy: "Do you respect Dr. B.? I respect Dr. C. Do you respect Dr. D.?"

LaVerne: "Yes."

Cindy: "Do you really respect Dr. D.? She never talks to me."

LaVerne: "I think so. I don't know her very well."

Cindy: "All right. End of conversation. Thank you. Oh, the judge was very unfair. When I spoke to him in person, he said he thought I should get away from my family; then in court he committed me for 30 days. He's a prejudiced hypocrite of a judge. I hate him!"

(A little later, the same day, I taped another conversation.)

Cindy: "Hello, Mommy thinks I'm sick, but I don't think I'm sick."

LaVerne: "Mommy thinks you're sweet."

Cindy: "Mommy thinks I'm sweet, but I don't think I'm sweet. Mommy is good to me. She brought me some candy, some pop and tacos and cigarettes (oops) and all kinds of things. And, oh, I appreciate everything she's done for me even though she thinks I don't."

LaVerne: "I know you appreciate it."

Cindy: "All right. Anything to say to the tape recorder, Mom?"

LaVerne: "Oh, boy, its hard to talk to a tape recorder. I sound just like Emerald."

Cindy: "Say something else."

LaVerne: "Cindy, I love you."

After this, I sang a song I had composed. It is written in a minor key with a very depressing melody. The words are as follows:

> All my life I've been persecuted for my Father's sake,
> And he grieves for me; he grieves for me.
> Jesus died on the cross for me, shed His blood for me,
> And I love Him so; I love Him so.
> Jesus soon is coming back for me; just you wait and see.
> He is coming back; He is coming back for me!

Cindy: "Dr. C. and the judge committed me, and it hasn't been fair. I went to court and Dr. C. testified against me saying that I had flight of ideas, talked 24 hours a day, spent too much time on the phone and had radical behavior; so high that I couldn't control myself, or so depressed that I was going to commit suicide. Which is more or less the same thing that Dr. A. said; more or less the same thing that Dr. C. said. I'm going to sue Dr. A. for $100,000. Lawyer Jim is going to be my attorney. I've been screwed over and over again. I'm suing for defamation of character, malpractice, prejudice and perjury!"

Mom and I sing a chorus together on the tape:

Father, I adore you,
Lay my life before you,
How I love you.

Cindy: "That was kind of nice, wasn't it? Don't we have beautiful singing voices? Ha! I bet we could be stars together, couldn't we? Mother and daughter. Oh, especially me, cuz I'm so talented. (chuckle) What are my talents?"

LaVerne: "Musical talent of playing the piano. Being sweet."

Cindy: "Yes, when I want to be."

LaVerne: "Being cute."

Cindy: "When I wanna be cute. Being talented in writing?"

LaVerne: "You write well."

Cindy: "How am I personality-wise?"

LaVerne: "Nice personality."

Cindy: "Looks-wise?"

LaVerne: "Very nice looking."

Cindy: "Weight-wise?"

LaVerne: "Just right."

Cindy: "Dancing-wise?"

LaVerne: "No good! (Both have a good laugh.)"

Cindy: "Singing-wise?"

LaVerne: "Average."

Cindy: "Piano playing?"

LaVerne: "Excellent to superior." (Mom and I sang another duet, "Gonna lay down my burdens, down by the riverside.")

Cindy: "I'm angry with society. I'm angry with my doctors. I'm angry with my judge. I'M ANGRY! But I'm not angry with my family anymore. I've had a bum rap ever since June 25, 1983, when my first doctor said that I had bipolar disorder. I'm going to clear it so that everybody realizes that I'm not sick. I'll take any measures at all to do what I have to do, no matter who I hurt; whether I hurt my mother, my father, my brothers, my sisters-in-law, my friends or anybody. I will do anything to clear my name because I'm sticking up for myself from now on. I have been tortured in the seclusion room. If you ever want to torture someone and make him go crazy, you put him in the torture chamber, otherwise known as the stabilization room!" (End of taped conversation.)

Chapter 14

MY ESCÁPE

Friday, October 14, 1983

After six weeks at Jamestown State Hospital, my fifth hearing took place in Fargo. As usual I was brought to court by a policeman and generally treated like the criminal that I was not.

The hearing was of short duration, but the consequences of this hearing dragged on and on. My Jamestown doctor testified that I was so much better. However, to make absolutely sure that I was stabilized on lithium, she recommended a short stay in another hospital. Of course, I was terribly upset when I heard that. I wanted out, right now!

My folks, unbeknownst to me, had already made arrangements for my admission to the United Hospital in Grand Forks.

I appeared to be very much better, but I was slipping from mania down into depression. I realize that now. However, at that time, the decision to extend my hospitalization again generated despair and the feeling that life was not worth living.

After the hearing I was taken back to jail to wait until some law enforcement officier could take me to Grand Forks. Mom drove ahead and waited for me at the hospital. It was about 9:00 p.m. when I arrived. We waited for another two hours or so until we were interviewed by another doctor, my fifth. This was the assistant doctor. He was going fishing next day, so he wanted to get the interview completed that night. I was upset by some of the things Mom said, and it took until 1:00 in the morning before it was over. I was totally miserable. I went to my room with a feeling of total despair and hopelessness.

Saturday, October 15, 1983

The next morning I slept late. I didn't want to get up or even live. It was fall, and that's the time I would get depressed each year. The lithium had helped the manic phase, but had not helped the depression yet. A nurse came in to tell me that my parents were on the phone, so I was forced to get up. They wondered if I would be all right if they didn't come to see me that day. That would be the first Saturday that Mom wouldn't be with me since I came back from New York. I assured them that I would be all right even though I was feeling terrible.

I hated this new place with new people. There was only one young girl there at the time; the others were older. There weren't even any cute boys to make it a little more interesting.

Sunday, October 16, 1983

On Sunday afternoon Mom and Dad came to visit. They tried to cheer me up, but nothing they said made me feel any better. I told them that one of my classmates was coming to see me that evening, so they decided to go home about suppertime. We spent the afternoon talking, trying to play pool or just sitting together in silence.

I walked with them to the door, and what I saw made my heart go a million miles an hour! The door was not locked! I could just walk out! I tried to hide my excitement as I gave them tight farewell hugs because I knew exactly what I was going to do. I was going to ESCAPE and get as far away from those hospitals as possible!

No one paid any attention to me as I rushed back to my room, put on some extra clothes and waited my chance to sneak out. It was so easy. Nobody was watching as I walked out the door, down the steps and out the hospital door to FREEDOM! I had no plans, of course. I just ran as fast as I could towards Perkins Cafe.

When I got to the highway, I hailed down a car. The first car I hailed, stopped but I was unlucky. The driver was another creep. His intentions were not good. He took me to a bar where I used some of my $40 for drinks.

The doctors had thought that I was so much better, but I was far from well at this point.

By the time I left the bar, inebriated, it was dark. I ran to the highway and again frantically hailed down the first semi that went by. The driver pulled over, and I jumped in, relieved that I could now get as far away from these horrible hospitals as I possibly could. California was as far as I could go, so that was my destination.

I was tired, drunk and sick. I fell asleep after awhile, and the next thing I knew I was looking into the big, bewhiskered face of this repulsive creature. I was unable to defend myself. It was a nightmare of terror and revulsion! When we arrived at Duluth, I jumped out of his truck and got out of his sight as quickly as possible.

I made a beeline to the phone and called home. I always called home, especially when something terrible had happened. I didn't tell them where I was or where I was going, but I let them know that I wasn't ever coming back to be put in those hospitals again.

Monday, October 17, 1983

From Duluth I hitched a ride with another truck driver. This man was nice, kind and decent. He did not take advantage of my vulnerability. He was going to California, and it was my intention to go with him all the way. However, I became so restless that I had to get off at Albuquerque, NM. Of course, I was not taking any of my medicine, and the effects of lithium were gone after the first 24 hours. For this reason the racing thoughts and inner restlessness were getting worse.

Wednesday, October 19, 1983
The third truck driver who gave me a ride to Fort Worth, Texas, was a scum, like the first driver. I couldn't suffer the trucks or the drivers any longer, so I decided to stay in Fort Worth.

Chapter 15

A MOTHER'S PERSPECTIVE

Friday, October 14, 1983

After the hearing I drove to United Hospital in Grand Forks to wait for Cindy. The admission interview lasted until 1:00 in the morning. As I left to go home, it eventually got through my foggy brain that the doors of this new psychiatric unit WERE NOT LOCKED! Stupidly, I prayed, "God, please don't let Cindy find out that the doors are open!" The staff had been warned that she would leave if given the opportunity. I gradually got over some of my concern by reasoning that since she was so much better, she wouldn't want to leave now.

Sunday, October 16, 1983

I did not visit Cindy on Saturday. I was getting so physically and mentally exhausted from all the stress and lack of sleep. She sounded pretty good when we talked to her, so I felt we could wait until Sunday.

I brought some of her music along when we went to visit her. She was playing the piano again. She seemed glad to see us, but it was obvious that she was getting depressed again. She played some of the classical pieces, and I was hoping that this would help her get through the days she would have to spend in this hospital. After awhile she told us that a classmate of hers was going to visit her that evening about 6:30 p.m. We were so glad to hear that! How wonderful that she was having a visitor. This had never happened before. We were overjoyed at that news. It was with a lighter step that we left the psychiatric unit this time. But the unlocked door and the fear that she might walk out lurked in the corner of my brain.

On our way home we stopped to eat and while there I called a pastor whom I knew and asked if he would visit Cindy. He promised that he would and also promised that some of the young people in his church would visit Cindy. I was so relieved and happy to hear him say that. I thought that finally things were getting better, and life would return to some form of normalcy. How wrong I was!

We had not been home for more than a few minutes when the phone rang. A voice stated in a matter-of-fact-tone, "This is the nurses' station. Cindy has left the unit." "O, God! Oh, my God! What can we do? When did she leave?" Our worst fears were now a reality! This nurse continued in the same toneless voice. "We have contacted the police." That was it. She showed not a trace of concern or regret that it had happened although I was in a state of shock, muttering, "Oh, my God!" over and over. This was the last straw, I thought, but of course it wasn't. I hung up the phone. I then called the police and got the same type of reception there. The impression I got was one of total indifference. I finally told the lady to please not use that sarcastic, impatient tone of voice as I was desperate. Then she didn't say anything, so I hung up knowing there would be no help coming from there. I called the nurses' station again to find out how it could have happened. Didn't the staff keep the patients who were elopement risks in pajamas or barefoot or take any measures to discourage patients from leaving? The nurse listened and then responded that at times they did, but as I was about to ask something else, she told me that she had a patient who needed attention. I said, "I'm sorry," and hung up. I was made to feel that I was bothering her and taking up her valuable time.

It was very easy to leave as the doors are located at the back of the nurses' station making it impossible for the staff to observe those who are leaving unless they happened to be going out themselves. Outside the doors there is only a corridor with no desk or station, so that anyone can enter or leave the unit unhindered. Whoever designed that psychiatric unit must not have known anything about bipolar disorder!

Monday, October 17, 1983

On Monday afternoon Cindy's doctor called, attempting to convince us that if someone doesn't WANT to take medication, there is no point in locking them up because they'll find a way of getting around it. They have to WANT to take the medication themselves. His philosophy was just what we had been fighting so desperately AGAINST. But what he said helped in that when Cindy called, we assured her that we would never put her in a hospital involuntarily again.

Tuesday, October 18, 1983

The next morning at five o'clock the phone rang. We both ran to the phone. It was Cindy! She was hitchhiking with truck drivers. In an expressionless voice she told us that she was on her way to New York to be a model. She knew that was about the worst thing she could tell us. As miserable as she felt, she wanted us to share in her misery. In her mind, even then, all her problems stemmed from the doctors and her family. I knew Cindy did not want to be a model, but she had been threatening to go back to New York all along.

She called in the evening again, thank God, so we knew she was alive. This time she talked to her brothers also. They tried to persuade her to tell us where she was really going, but she stuck to her story. Every day while hitchhiking, she would call, sometimes two or three times a day. Her calls kept us from total collapse.

Thursday, October 20, 1983

On Thursday she arrived at her destination. After two or three phone calls from this place, Jeff was able to persuade her to tell us where she was, so that we could send her some clothes and a little money. By now she was getting more depressed. Her money was long gone, so with the promise from us that we wouldn't do anything to try to get her back home, she let us know that she was in Fort Worth, Texas. We suggested that she find a Gospel Mission and live there until she found a job. Next day she called, giving us her address. I packed some clothes and put $30 in a Bible to send. We didn't dare send much money as we just didn't know what she would do.

Monday, October 24, 1983

Cindy didn't call us for two days, so I called the mission and was told that she had left. It was getting almost too much to endure, but falling to pieces wouldn't help Cindy. She was our only concern. Our prayers were answered as she called the next day. She told us that she had found a job as a parking lot attendant, but she didn't know if she could handle sitting in that little cubicle as she was restless and didn't want to be boxed in like in the institution. We told her that we had sent clothes and a little money to the mission. She went back to the mission and picked up the clothes, but gave most of them away to those less fortunate who were staying there.

Thursday, October 27, 1983

Cindy had given us the address, but not the name, of the parking lot where she was working. I had the telephone company find the name for us. I then called the parking lot but found that she was not working there! I was getting into a state of panic imagining the worst. Where was she getting the money to eat? Where was she sleeping? No car this time. She had left the mission again. I remembered the telephone calls she had been getting from New York while I was staying with her in Fargo. I answered one of these calls and pretended to be

Cindy's roommate. The caller said that she hadn't met Cindy while she was in New York, but that Lawyer Jim had told her about Cindy. I asked if Jim was the boy at Port Authority, and she responded by laughing hilariously and saying, "Well, yes, I would think that he does consider himself a BOY!" She said that she was getting ready for a beauty contest and was having a great time. I should be sure to tell Cindy!

Ironically, this very day in Fort Worth Cindy made a call to this "snake in the grass" in New York.

Chapter 16

FORT WORTH, TEXAS

Thursday, October 20, 1983

The truck driver dropped me off on the outskirts of town. As I was walking down the road, I started crying as I was without money and getting more depressed. After awhile, I stopped at a motel filled with guys attending some sporting event. I sat down in the lobby to rest. Then I called home as I always did.

I did not tell them where I was, but Mom suggested that I find a Gospel Mission. I didn't know what else to do, so I took her advice. It was getting dark, and I had no idea where I was or how to get to the mission. Also, I was so hungry and was wishing that I had money to go into the nice restaurant for a meal. I couldn't do that, so eventually I asked one of the men where the Gospel Mission was. He was very kind and offered to give me a ride there. He took me right to the door. I was so grateful. I was glad for a bed that night, even though there were 20 beds in one room.

Friday, October 21, 1983

After getting up, I called home again as I was always compelled to do. I talked to my brother, Jeff, who begged me to reveal my location so that they could send me money and clothes. That sounded good, so I told him but, before I was able to get the clothes and money from home, I was kicked out the mission. I had refused to fix my bed and do other required chores, and that was not tolerated. I was forced to go back to the streets again. There seems little doubt that they thought I was on drugs and were unaware that I was sick.

After a few days, I did go back for the clothes, and they were so nice and friendly to me, and assured me that I could stay. I guess when Mom had called and learned that I wasn't there, she told them about my sickness.

Monday, October 24, 1983

I found a job as a parking lot attendant for $4 an hour. When it came time to go to work, I just couldn't get myself to go into the little boxlike building, so I never went to work.

I was starving. I only had a few cents left, not enough to buy a candy bar. I walked into the Americana Motel to apply for a waitress job. Applications were being taken downstairs in a big room. I filled out the application form and then went back upstairs.

In the lobby I saw candy bars, and I wanted a Butterfinger so badly. I checked to see how much money I had. I counted and I was only about 12 cents short. I had more money than I thought. I asked the clerk if she would sell a bar for that as it was all the money I had. She gave me a puzzled look and refused. I hung around; when the cashier wasn't looking, I grabbed a Butterfinger.

It is difficult for me to tell these things because what I did was so against everything that I believed and held sacred. The illness had made me beg, steal and lie. God knows my heart, and He knows that, had I been well, I would never have stooped to this and all the other bizarre things that I did.

I hurried to the bathroom with the bar and ate it in about three bites. I was still very hungry, so I watched my chance to take another candy bar. This time I heard someone say, "She took another candy bar!" I took off down the steps to the room where I had just applied for a job and sat down as though nothing was wrong. Then the telephone rang. The person who answered it looked in my direction, so I thought that I had better get out of there fast! I ran out of the building with visions of cops pursuing me to take me back to jail. I was shaking like a leaf.

I couldn't go back to the mission so I kept walking. A guy and girl in a little sports car asked if I wanted a ride. Of course I did. They lived in a dingy apartment. I walked with his girlfriend to wash clothes at a laundromat.

They introduced me to another scum bum who asked me to go for a ride with him. He took me out to his trailer house on the outskirts of the city. Fortunately, his roommate was a nice, mild-mannered hillbilly. He was not threatening like the creep who had brought me out there. I asked his roommate if he would take me back to the city. He not only took me back to town but when I asked if he would buy me a couple of much needed items of clothing, he responded, "Shore thing!" He paid for the items, and I thanked him profusely and told him how nice he was. He hadn't even tried to take advantage of me. Then he left me on the sidewalk in front of the clothing store.

I hadn't called home for a couple of days or so, and my folks had no idea where I had gone. I decided to call home. When I did, Mom told me that the clothes and money they had sent were at the Gospel Mission, so I should go back there to get them. Getting some money was the big drawing card.

I found my way back to the mission, and looked for the money first. There in the Bible, I found only $30. What a letdown! Well, at least I could buy a few meals. I had met another street person named Randy at the mission. We hung around together, so I told him that he could come with me, and I'd pay for some food. The 30 dollars was gone the same day that I got it. But now I wasn't hungry! The Gospel Mission staff told me I could stay so, with nothing better to do, I stayed.

Wednesday, October 26, 1983

There were many interesting and pathetic people staying at the mission. Two homosexual girls claimed they were going to get married. One of them was pregnant and told me she was so happy they were going to have a baby. She was going to teach her kid to be a "Butch." I still had enough sense to feel sorry for the baby being born under such awful circumstances.

Everyone at the mission was looking for work. One of the girls had just gotten out of the Hare Krishna cult. Her parents wouldn't let her come home. Her name was Karen and she wanted work desperately. She did finally get a job as a nanny for 50 dollars a week. I felt so bad that her parents wouldn't let her return home; but, strangely enough, I did not think of going home to my parents who would have welcomed me back with open arms!

About a block or so behind the mission house there was a steep cliff overlooking a freeway. Some of us went there to talk and others to smoke pot or whatever. A guy came rolling in on his Harley-Davidson bike. He had the black leather jacket outfit and a gold pendant hanging around his neck, looking like some big gang leader. He started talking to me. I asked about the pendant. He said that he was into devil worship. He called his religion, the Arts. He said that once in this cult, it is hard to get out, and admitted that he felt trapped. Although it was getting dark, and I was surrounded by creeps, on the dangerous edge of a cliff with a sheer drop to the freeway below, I wasn't scared. Curfew was 10 p.m. at the mission, so those of us living there dragged ourselves back just in time.

One person meant well when he told my folks that they shouldn't be so worried about me because there is a sub-culture in our society that accepts and protects the misfits. The 'accepts' part was right, but none of us were capable of protecting ourselves, much less someone else.

Thursday, October 27, 1983

The next day some of us went to a bar a block away where we talked in guarded tones about the big conspiracy of big business and the end of the world. Some of us had the same delusions, our thinking was in perfect sync. They were mentally ill, just as I was, though we thought that we were well as fish, and everyone else was strange.

I hated Fort Worth, but I loved New York City. No doubt my being manic in New York and my becoming more depressed while here was the reason. My big passion was still to help make a better world. I thought that I would write a screenplay since I believed that I was very creative. I was having delusions of grandeur.

I was broke. That was reality. I was tired of being broke! While pondering this reality, a brilliant idea hit me. I would call Lawyer Jim in New York and ask him for money. I knew he wanted me back there because he had been calling me ever since I left New York. He called me at my apartment and at the institution, trying to lure me back to New York City. No sooner thought than done.

I went to a pay phone and called. He actually answered the phone. When I told him who was calling, he started yelling with feigned concern, "Where have you been? Why haven't I heard from you?" After explaining to him that I hadn't had a chance, I got up the courage to ask him for money to get back to New York. Without hesitation, he said, "Come by plane!" I didn't want to seem too greedy, so I said that bus fare would be good enough. I thought asking for a smaller amount would ensure his sending the money. Now I know that he would have sent the money for an airplane ticket, but I wasn't going to take a chance. He was very eager for me to come back, and the reason should have been crystal clear, but at that time I was naive beyond belief. After awhile, he called the mission to make sure that I really was there. When he was satified that I was telling the truth, he telegraphed $100 to me. He assured me that he would be waiting for me at Port Authority. It was just like the stories I had read about girls being picked up by pimps in the bus station on the Minnesota Strip.

Money again. It felt good. Randy and I went to a restaurant for a big meal. We had been planning to go to Colorado, but that meal took a big bite out the hundred. That night we stayed at a Super 8 Motel. There were two big beds, and I let Randy know that I was paying for the room, so he had better stay away from me. He did. With two people spending, that $100 didn't last long. Now we definitely couldn't go to Colorado.

Friday, October 28, 1983

The next day another brilliant idea struck me. It had worked so well with Lawyer Jim that it would surely work again. I'd call home to the folks and tell them I wanted to come home. Then I'd ask them to buy an airplane ticket which I would cash. That should be good for a couple of hundred at least. Randy and I would get to Colorado yet. I knew my folks would not send that much money, but a ticket home; they'd buy that! What I didn't know was that a ticket could not be cashed in.

I made that fateful call to Mom in the afternoon, and gave her the news. "Mom, I want to come home!" I said. She was so-o-o happy, and told me that she would go immediately to buy the ticket. I could hardly wait to call back in the evening to find out how much the ticket had cost. At about six that evening, I called back. "Mom, did you get the ticket?" I asked eagerly. Mom said, "Yes, I did. The flight is out of Dallas tomorrow." My next question, which I could not resist asking, spilled the beans. "How much was the ticket?" Mom then realized that all I wanted was the money. With disappointment in her voice, she informed me that the ticket could not be cashed. That did it! I screamed, "Keep the ticket! I don't want it!" I slammed down the receiver, frustrated and angry. What was I going to do now?

I didn't know that God was working to answer all those prayers for me. He saw the end of all this and was in control.

Saturday, October 29, 1983

Next morning, I went to the Dallas Airport to check for sure about the ticket as Mom said that she was sending it anyway. Maybe she was mistaken, or just told me that to discourage me from cashing it. I asked for a ride from one of the workers at the mission to the bus station where I could catch a bus to Dallas. Somehow, I made it to the Dallas Airpot. I asked about the ticket. It was there, but they did NOT cash tickets. Then I asked if I could change the destination to Denver, Colorado. The answer was, "No!" I was supposed to use the ticket right away, this very day, but I couldn't make up my mind that fast. I had no intention of going home, but what else could I do? I took the shuttle bus to the motel, just following the crowd.

When I got to the motel, I realized that I didn't have money for a room. I called home, but my folks weren't home. That was the first time I had called and not been able to get them by phone. Where were they? How could they leave home when I needed to talk to them. I depended on their being home every time I called. I almost panicked, but I called Lonnie, and he was there. I told him that I was broke and didn't know where I would sleep that night. Lonnie told me not to worry; he would get me a room at the motel and put it on his Visa card. He asked me to get the clerk on the phone. I heard her side of the conversation and realized that she couldn't accept Lonnie's Visa over the phone. I started crying in desperation, and I was crying so loudly that I attracted the attention of a pilot who was passing by. He asked me what was wrong. In between sobs I told him that I didn't have any money, and I didn't have any place to sleep that night. In a kind and gentle voice he said, "Don't cry. I will pay for a room here and a meal." After making arrangements, he left as suddenly as he appeared. I can't remember if I even said thank you.

I certainly had been broke without a place to sleep before this, so why did I react the way I did this time, crying my eyes out? My situation was not as hopeless as it had been many times before, and I had the plane ticket to take me home. Still, I couldn't stop crying.

I have since learned that the reason I couldn't get my folks by phone that night was that they had gone to special meetings in a neighboring town. That very night there was special prayer for me. They prayed that I would use the ticket and come home. God answered their prayers!

Sunday, October 30, 1983

I was awakened by a call from Mom the next morning. She told me they would meet me in Bemidji that evening. I wanted to sleep longer, so I said that I would be there and hurried her off the phone.

Miraculously, I was up in plenty of time for getting to the Dallas Airport. When it was time to board the plane. I had another big, stressful time. The ticket had been bought for a Saturday flight, which was cheaper than a Sunday flight. I didn't have the additional money needed. I called Lonnie again, telling him that I couldn't use the ticket. He told me not to worry! (Where had I heard that before?) He would see to it that I could take that flight home. And he did! No more questions were asked, and I was allowed to board the plane.

There was a stop in Minneapolis. Mom therefore arranged that my aunt and her husband were there to take me to lunch, so that I wouldn't be tempted to take off!

We landed in Bemidji at 9 p.m. I hadn't planned to come home, and everything had happened so fast that, when I saw my folks, I was frustrated. The first thing I did was to pick a fight with Lonnie about something unimportant. I could not understand that anyone had suffered because of me. I was sick, but I still did not believe that there was a thing wrong with me, in spite of everything I had done. To me, it made perfect sense. I was well and everyone else's thinking was off kilter. I was argumentative and unreasonable.

Chapter 17

A MOTHER'S PERSPECTIVE

Friday, October 28, 1983

This particular Friday I was getting to be a basket case. I was at work, but I could not concentrate. Someone had recommended that I call a Christian psychiatrist at Golden Valley, so I called and was able to talk to him. I told him that we thought our daughter was in Fort Worth, but by now she may have gone to Denver, Colorado. What should we do? How dangerous was this? He recommended that we do all we could to find her and bring her home because her situation was extremely dangerous. He tried to be as tactful as he could; not like the psychiatrist I had called when Cindy had gone to New York, who told me that we would find her either in a hospital, in jail, or . . ., just stopping short of saying a morgue. Even so, the pressure was mounting. Cindy needed to be found and brought home. I had called the police in Fort Worth and also the Denver police, to no avail. I just had to try to do something. As the morning progressed, I was so uneasy and nervous that I felt I just had to talk to someone who understood the illness. At that time there was a psychologist in a neighboring town. I told the other staff members that I needed to talk to him, as I felt that I just couldn't get through the day.

After telling the psychologist a little about the situation, his recommendation was the same, "Do all you can to find her and bring her home!" His words intensified the urgency I was feeling.

I went back to work with a knot in my stomach and a pain in my chest. "God, please help us!" I pleaded. My prayers were just panicky cries to God for help. I couldn't formulate a prayer for any length because I was getting too distracted. It was again beginning to seem hopeless. We had promised that we would never again put her in a hospital against her will. "Please, God, perform another miracle for our precious Cindy!"

At about 2 p.m. God answered that prayer. The phone rang. I lifted the receiver and heard, "Hi, Mom, I want to come home!" I was elated, relieved, thankful, overcome with emotion. I could hardly answer, but I told her that I would go to Thief River for an airline ticket, right away. She would have it the next day. I hung up the receiver, rejoicing! I rushed to buy the ticket. It crossed my mind that perhaps she had in mind to cash the ticket, so I asked if that was possible, and it wasn't, fortunately. I was back home by about 4:30 p.m. to wait for Cindy's call.

She didn't call back until about six in the evening. Everything was wonderful until she asked how much the trip home would cost. I knew then she just wanted the money, so I told her that the ticket could not be cashed. She ended up screaming that we forget it; she didn't want the ticket. The highs and lows I was experiencing were almost bipolar. But God was in control of it all, working His will and way with Cindy.

Saturday, October 29, 1983

Saturday evening Oscar and I went for counseling and to special meetings in a neighboring town. Two pastors together with others prayed that Cindy would use the ticket to come home and that God would continue to lead and protect. These prayers caused Cindy to holler and cry, and you've read the rest in Cindy's account.

Sunday, October 30, 1983

Cindy came home, She was irritable, argumentative, frustrated and unhappy, but she was home. She stayed until November 10, 1983. We took her to Fargo to look for work and an apartment. By November 11th she had found a job as a waitress and had an apartment which she shared with a roommate.

I had given her the book, *Mood Swings*, to read, but it just made her angry. She couldn't understand how we could think she had the illness described in the book. However, she went to a doctor in Thief River for a prescription of lithium. She started taking lithium on her own 11 days after coming home.

Friday, November 11, 1983

Five days after she had moved into her shared apartment, her roommate's boyfriend came back to town and wanted to move in.

Thursday, November 17, 1983

Cindy started her waitress job on Thursday. When she came back to the apartment after her first day of work, she found out that the boyfriend was moving in for sure. She called home to tell us that she had to get out that very day. I told her I would try to find a place on a temporary basis and would call back as soon as possible.

I called a cousin or two, but due to circumstances, that was not possible. I called Cindy back and told her to go to the YWCA, for the night anyway. She hated to do that, but there was no other choice. If she hadn't had a job, she could have come home.

Friday, November 18, 1983

At about 7 p.m. as I was thinking about Cindy and wondering how she was doing at work, the phone rang. When

I answered, I heard the same familiar sound of crying and the words, "Mom, I'm in jail again!! They handcuffed me and brought me here and won't even let me have a cigarette. Mom, I can't stand this anymore! I can't take it in the hospital again! Can't you do something? P-l-e-a-s-e!" Each syllable was punctuated with a sob. I was crying right with her. We weren't prepared for this. Her brothers had warned her that this might happen, but considering the indifference shown by the authorities up to this point, we thought the chance of this happening was negligible.

"Cindy, I'm so sorry. You know we had nothing to do with this." "Yes, I know that, but there must be something you can do. They are taking me back to the State Hospital, Mom! I just can't go back there again!" I said, "Cindy, Dad and I will come tomorrow, and I will call the state's attorney to see what can be done. I'll call you as soon as I find out anything. I love you Cindy!"

With a heavy heart I called until I got the state's attorney on the phone. He assured me that he would not oppose Cindy's release from the hospital if that was what we wanted, and if the doctor agreed. Next, I called until I got Cindy's attorney on the phone, and told him that we didn't want Cindy back in the hospital. His response was, "Good, I'll put you on the stand." Then I called Cindy back to let her know that she would not have to stay in the hospital.

She ended up staying in the hospital five days until her sixth hearing set for Wednesday morning, November 23rd.

Wednesday, November 23, 1983

On the day before Thanksgiving, Cindy had her final mental health hearing.

On the way to this hearing I called one of the places where Cindy had applied for work on the chance that there might be an opening. I wanted to have the encouragement for Cindy, and I wanted to be able to tell the judge that she had a job waiting for her.

The answer I got from the manager was, "Yes, there's an opening. I tried to get her by phone yesterday, but she wasn't at home." What terrific news! I fairly flew up the steps of the courthouse. The hearing was brief. The doctor recommended to the judge that she be under court jurisdiction for up to 90 days as an OUT-patient.

Cindy and I spent the rest of the day calling around for an apartment. By 6 p.m. we had found a one-room apartment. We both breathed a sigh of relief as we drove home. Maybe there was hope for the future.

Chapter 18

MY WORST FEAR

(Cindy) Sunday, October 30, 1983

I was home, but not happy. Any mention of my being sick and needing lithium would set me off. Mom gave me a book, *Mood Swings*, to read. I couldn't concentrate enough to read more than a little here and there, but it made me angry to think that Mom and Dad felt I was like the people in this book. She also told me stories such as the one about my aunt's neighbor boy in Minneapolis. He took off on his motorcycle in a manic state. He would call home crying, but every time his folks asked him where he was, he would never tell. He acted as if he wanted to come home, but would never let them help him get back home. Somehow, they did find him, halfway across the contry. His brother fought with him and physically forced him home. Now he was taking lithium and was fine. I just couldn't see any similarity. I didn't want to listen to that garbage. I was NOT sick. I was not like that guy.

I was so anxious to get back to Fargo. I couldn't stand staying home. My judgment was becoming less impaired as I got more depressed and this may have been the reason for my going to a doctor to get some lithium.

Mom would take me to Fargo now and again, to look for an apartment. I found waitress job, but it lasted only one night. I found an apartment, but that lasted only five days. I ended up at the YWCA which I hated. It was like being back at the Gospel Mission in Fort Worth.

Friday, November 18, 1983

My second day of work I slept too late at the Y, and there was no time to look for another apartment before work, which was 6 p.m. Old Broadway cafe was close by, so I went there just for something to do before going to work. I sat at the bar, drinking a coke, when a man and woman came up to me, one on each side. They showed their badges, and informed me that I was under arrest! Under arrest?!! I became hysterical. Just the thought of going to jail or hospital to be locked up again made me frantic. I screamed and fought like a banshee as they dragged me out. The people in the bar thought it was a big joke. It was a cruel joke, and they were cruel people.

My worst fear had just become a reality. I was in jail again. Why? Why? The lady cop explained to me that I had been picked up because I had left the Grand Fork's hospital without permission while I was still under a court order.

I told her that I had to be at work at 6 p.m. She said she would call my employer. I heard her on the phone saying, "Cindy can't come to work tonight." There was a pause. Then she continued, "It might be a couple of months." I died inside when I heard those horrifying words. I couldn't take much more of this.

I called home, and you have read about that. I was taken back to Jamestown that same night to await another hearing. At Jamestown everyone seemed happy to see me. The staff members thought that I was so much better. My doctor was ready to recommend that I be an outpatient. I didn't mind it so much this time because I was able to sleep. What no one seemed to understand was that my improved appearance and behavior was due to my judgment and insight returning as I became more and more depressed.

Another reason why it was bearable this time was that I knew the doctor, my lawyer and my folks were all in agreement that I shuld be an outpatient, so I was not in such a panic about the hearing.

Wednesday, November 23, 1983
The court hearing was short, and for the first time everyone testified in my favor! I left the courtroom for the last time.

Six months since I came back from New York; six doctors; six weeks in Jamestown before; now six days — that evil number again. Hum-m-m! Oh, well, no more dwelling on the significance of numbers, letters or names, such as had occupied my thoughts when manic.

This day was filled with good news. I had a part-time job at a Stop and Go convenience store, thanks to my ever-lovin' Mom. I also found an apartment. Mom and I drove home feeling much better about life.

Thursday, November 24, 1983

It was Thanksgiving Day, and we were invited to Lonnie and Jan's for dinner. Everyone had been through so much with me and with losing the businesses; it was more of a strained than a happy time.

Friday, November 25, 1983

Mom took me to Fargo for my first day of work at the convenience store.

Chapter 19

A MOTHER'S PERSPECTIVE

Tuesday, November 22, 1983

We should have known that Cindy would not want to come home after her few days at the state hospital, but we thought that she might want to spend a few days with us until she found another apartment and job. As Grand Forks was closer to home we drove there to the same hospital from which she had eloped, to ask if her doctor there would accept her as an outpatient. Would we never learn?

He told us that he could not agree to treat her on an outpatient basis while she was under court order, and while she was unwilling to admit that she was sick and needed lithium. He stated that it was his belief that it doesn't do a person any good to be locked up if she is not going to cooperate. He didn't want to have to report her to the authorities when or if she did not come for appointments. He also gave his opinion about our sending money to her for the airfare home. He thought that we should have sent her just enough money for bus fare. Things shouldn't be made too easy for her. What he didn't know about manic-depressives! By now, even we knew that if she had taken a bus, she probably would have stayed in whatever city took her fancy, and we would have had to go through more weeks or months of torture. Moreover, there was the possiblity that she might never have come home at all!

I asked him what to do if she continued to refuse to take lithium. He replied, "Well, there are casualties, of course." We had heard enough! As we left the office, I was absolutely certain of one thing — Cindy would NOT be one of his casualties! We were sent a bill for this office call which we refused to pay, and told him the reason why. It was his hospital from which she eloped and his staff treated us shabbily afterwards. Neither the doctor nor his staff had expressed any regret about Cindy's eloping. He could be happy that we didn't sue!

It was getting late in the afternoon, and we needed to find a doctor who would accept Cindy as his patient. From the hospital lobby I called Fargo, and late as it was, there was a doctor. He listened to my brief summary of events and agreed to taking her on as a patient, if she was released as an outpatient at the hearing. We were so relieved by this.

Chapter 20

THE COLD, COLD WINTER

(Cindy) December, 1983

I thought that I could finally start living again. I seemed to feel much better at first. I had a job, an apartment, my family and a new doctor to watch over me. What else did I need?

Still, as the weather got colder, I started sinking into the bottomless pit of despair and hopelessness. I wanted to sleep all the time. I had no interest in people, my job or life itself. If someone by some miracle would stop over, I would not open the door.

Somehow Peter learned I was back in town and would stop by, but I wouldn't open the door. My eyes were now open to see what a scuz ball he really was, and I didn't want anything to do with him. Also gone was the obsession for another man I had met the summer before I went to New York. He had been the object of all my mixed-up thoughts. At the time, I imagined that I was in love and couldn't live without him. I called him long distance from New York and Fort Worth and everywhere in between. How embarrassing to have thrown myself at him like that. I just feel like crying when I think of all the things that I have done and said because of this terrible illness.

I had told Mom that if I ever got depressed again, I would know that I was bipolar.

Christmas, 1983

Wel-l-, by Christmas I finally knew beyond a shadow of a doubt that I was definitely suffering from this diabolical disorder. I could hardly get out of bed. Taking a shower, dressing, combing my hair became almost impossible tasks. It was hard to lift my arm to comb my hair. Mom came to be with me every weekend, and sometimes during the week when I was especially sick.

Because I had run up such an exorbitant phone bill, I did not even have a phone. I had to go to an outside phone by a store to call home. Somehow, in spite of all this, I managed to keep my job working three or four nights a week. I guess I appeared fine to others, but they couldn't know the turmoil and fear that I was experiencing. I was not at all comfortable with people; yet I managed to wait on them and appear pleasant. I had been taking lithium regularly, but it didn't seem to be helping.

Mom spent her vacation with me. It was the coldest, most miserable and desolate Christmas ever! It was so cold that even though the van was plugged in, it would not start. We managed to get home for Christmas Eve and Christmas Day, but we had to go back for work.

Mom talked to my doctor about getting worse instead of better, but all he could say was that lithium works for the manic side and not the depressed side.

On New Year's Eve we came home again, but I had to work New Year's Day evening shift, so I had to go right back. Mom wasn't coming back with me, and I just didn't know how I could make it back to Fargo by myself. After traveling alone to Nashville, New York and hitchhiking to Fort Worth, alone, I didn't think I could drive 150 miles back to Fargo by myself. Unreal! But that was the case with me now.

Anyway, I asked my folks if they would drive behind me for a while until I got going. I stopped in the next town and asked if they would go just a little further with me. Each time I stopped, I'd beg, "Just one more town." This went on until they had followed me all the way back to Fargo and to my place of work! I hugged and thanked my folks profusely, and then with fear and trembling, I went to work. The depressed side of the disorder was showing its ugly face.

January-February 1984

These months dragged by with my sleeping, my writing, my working and my mom coming and going every week. I did look forward to her coming. That was ALL that I had to look forward to. The anti-depressant (imipramine) that I was taking just wasn't helping at this point.

March, 1984

I was beginning to feel better with more energy and a little more hope. I was escalating into a manic state again and didn't realize it.

I started making plans for the future. I wanted to re-apply at the same church college, but I gave up that idea and went back to business college instead. We all thought that the medicine was finally working.

I started going to the parks to sit and look at the grass, trees and little animals scampering about. Everything looked so fresh and beautiful. I was entranced by the beauty of the shimmering leaves in the sun. I felt so in tune with nature. It was an exhilarating and delicious feeling. It made me forget the horrible winter I had just gone through.

Monday, April 2, 1984

I entered business college again. At first it went all right. I was able to handle the classes and work, but as the weeks went by, I began to have trouble concentrating. It wasn't long before I started having the racing thoughts, restlessness and all the other rotten symptoms of the manic side. I was even hallucinating. I'm sure my classmates thought that my problem was drugs.

I started having trouble at work too. I couldn't figure out the sales. I had been doing this bookwork for months, but now it was impossible to do. I was in a daze. When I called home from work, Mom could tell by my talk that I was getting manic.

She came right down and went to my doctor to try to get some explanation for the medicine not working. He thought that it was just an episode that I was experiencing, and he decided to give me some haloperidol (Haldol) to get me through this episode. This is a miracle drug for most people, but it made me worse, much worse. I was being jerked up into psychoses. In addition to everything else, I now had headaches, diarrhea and nausea.

May, 1984

One very cold night in May I was forced to take my bike to work as my car had a flat tire. My judgment was affected again, so it never dawned on me to take a taxi on this cold, snowy night instead of riding my bike for five miles.

When closing time came, I was unable to do the bookwork, so I had to leave it undone. Mom had told me to take a taxi home, but by 11:30 p.m. I had forgotten that. Anyway, I was too restless. I needed to bike.

I got on my bike and intended to go home, but some guy in a car stopped me. He wanted to give me a ride home, but I refused. Then he said, "I have a bike at home. I'll put your bike in my trunk; then we'll go to my house, pick up my bike and we'll ride together." That sounded fine to me, so I agreed. I didn't know what he had in mind even though it was as plain as the nose on his face. He did get his bike, and we biked to Lindenwood Park where I learned what he had in mind. When he realized that I was not interested, he took off on his bike as fast as he could. I followed, but at a four-way stop, I rammed into the side of a car. I flew off my bike and landed with a thud. The guy in the car stopped to ask if I was okay?

I told him that I was, and he drove off. I was badly bruised, but no broken bones.

I was doing bizarre things such as buying a bird and letting it fly all over my apartment. When my brother came to the apartment, it flew right by his face and almost scared him to death.

I could hear voices now that seemed so real to me. Demons were very real to me. They told me that I had committed the unpardonable sin, and that I belonged to the devil. The words I remember were, "Cindy, you've done it now; you're mine, and there's no turning back!" This terrified me; yet I placed all my brass candles and trinkets on my coffee table in a way which appeared to me to be an altar to the devil.

When my mother came the next day, I gave her a bag full of all the stuff that had an appearance of evil, and told her to take it right out to the dumpster. I wanted it out of the apartment. I called it Pandora's Box. I had placed tapes, my writings, marijuana and trinklets in it. Mom was glad to throw it away. Then she took the candles and put them back in place.

Thursday, May 10, 1984

On Thursday of the next week I was so ill that Mom came down to take me to the doctor. When I got to his office, I was so sick that I didn't really understand what was going on, and I sat with my eyes closed. The psychiatrist and his nurse talked as though nothing much was wrong. He repeated that it was an episode that I would get through. He even seemed to think that I could go to work the next day. He had no idea of what I was going through. If doctors don't understand, how can we expect others to understand?

May 12, 1984

Saturday, Mom called the psychiatrist on call. God certainly was watching over me as the doctor on call was Dr. John

Jamieson. He treated me like a human being who was really suffering. He seemed to understand what I was going through and gave me the kindness, understanding and encouragement that I so badly needed. This time I wanted to be admitted to the hospital in the worst way. Fortunately, my folks now had insurance, so I was allowed treatment at St. Luke's, the best hospital by far.

Dr. Jamieson told us that my irrational thinking and bizarre behavior were typical. He gave me hope that there was help. Words can't express how much his optimistic attitude and kindness helped all of us.

Chapter 21

A MOTHER'S PERSPECTIVE

May, 1984

When Cindy started getting better around Easter, I was confident that lithium was finally working for her. However, I noticed that she was talking fast and making some unrealistic plans, such as going to college in Virginia. This gave me pause to wonder, and I asked Oscar what he thought of this. Wishful thinking, I suppose, caused us to talk ourselves into believing that this was just Cindy's normal personality.

It was not long before we realized that this was not Cindy's usual self. She started calling more often, during the day as well as in the evening. Cindy was concerned about it herself as she told us that she was feeling too good, the first indication.

Tuesday, May 8, 1984

Cindy called, and her call scared us all so much that I rushed to Fargo arriving at about one in the morning to find her sitting on the couch puzzling over a parable that she was attempting to write. Ordinarily, she writes very well. It was about the egg, and how it represented the Trinity, but she couldn't figure out what the three parts of the egg were. "What are the three parts of an egg, Mom?" The shell, the yolk and what else?" I told her it was the egg white. She responded, "Oh, yah, for dumb! The egg white represents the Holy Spirit — three in one!" Cindy is intelligent, but the things she wrote when she was in a manic state just didn't make sense. She was aware of that and told me, "That doesn't make sense, does it?" Her thinking was confused, and she knew it now. Her doctor had increased her lithium and had prescribed a small dose of Haldol which was supposed to help her get over this bad episode, but it made her worse.

Wednesday, May 9, 1984

The next day she told me to write down how she felt, so that I could report it to the doctor. She said, "I can't concentrate. My thinking is confused. I can't remember what I've said. Disorganized. No attention span. I don't want friends. I'm beginning to question my values again, and I know they are right. I'm afraid my priorities are going to be bad again. I'm afraid I'll quit school again. I can't sleep much again. I'm obsessed with learning and logic. Details are so important to me. I'm back to writing all the time. Racing thoughts. Nervous and frustrated; yet I appear calm to others. I'm talking too much again. I want to understand my illness so desperately, but it's so hard to be open-minded. My appetite has changed to no appetite. I have diarrhea most of the time. Slightly nauseated all the time. Slight headaches that come and go. I'm not as concerned about my appearance as I should be. Sometimes I feel as though I'm going crazy. I don't understand the way I think!"

That should have been enough to send me pounding on the doctor's door in panic right then and there. I guess I'd become numb by all the misery Cindy and the whole family had been enduring. I don't know why, but we waited until her appointment.

Thursday, May 10, 1984

I took Cindy to her appointment hoping that her doctor would have some answers. I told him everything including the fact that she had driven on the wrong side of the street. He didn't seem too concerned about all of this. He called it an episode.

It had been six months since Cindy became his patient. During this time she had gone through suicidal depression and now mania, which we all feared, including Cindy. The impression I was given was that there was nothing to do now but wait and see. It had been almost a year since she had gone to New York. How long must we wait? How much longer could Cindy take the suffering.

Saturday, May 12, 1984

Cindy was extremely restless after a restless night. I had to rock her in my arms for her to sleep at all. In the afternoon we went to West Acres Shopping Center. She couldn't stand it there so we left. On our way home Cindy was so agitated and restless that I had to stop the car so that she could walk for awhile. After some time we got back in the car again. Then, in a tone and manner similar to slow motion as seen on television, Cindy said "This . . . . can't . . . . go . . . . on!" My heart started to pound! It was Saturday, and I wondered how I was going to get help for her on Saturday. I asked Cindy if she wanted to go to the hospital. Her answer was an emphatic, "Yes, YES!"

I took her back to the apartment and told her to try to rest while I went to the pay phone a block away to call the psychiatrist on call that day. I got through to the receptionist who said that the psychiatrist was on another phone, but would call back. I gave her the number of the pay phone. I didn't know that these phones didn't work for incoming calls. I ran back to the apartment to see how Cindy was. She was there, so I ran back to the pay phone. I waited a little while, but no call was forthcoming. I dialed the number again, and this time the doctor was there. He had tried to call, but the call didn't get through.

After explaining her symptoms and telling him the medication she was taking, he said, "Take all medicine away from her." I was shocked. We had tried to get her to take the lithium for months, and now that she was finally taking it, I should take it away from her?! "How can I do that?" I asked. He replied firmly, "Because I said that you should!" I asked him if lithium didn't work for Cindy, what medicine could be used, and he replied, "Tegretol (carbamazepine)." He asked if she wanted to come to the hospital, and I assured him that she did. Then he said to bring her to the emergency entrance of St. Luke's. Thank God, Oscar had Blue Cross/Blue Shield insurance by now.

This doctor is Dr. John Jamieson to whom we have dedicated our book. He had the warmth, understanding and real interest that put us at ease. Although he is extremely busy, working with medical students and having a full patient load, he took Cindy as his patient. We are so thankful to him.

Cindy was hospitalized this Saturday. She got there "just in time" as Cindy herself put it.

Chapter 22

PSYCHOTIC

(Cindy) Saturday, May 12, 1984

Entering 2 North at St. Luke's this time was quite different from the last time. I was so happy to be in the hospital now. I needed help and I knew it. I entered willingly and eagerly. The symptoms I was experiencing were horrible. I didn't want to live. I felt so evil, and I believed that I had committed the unpardonable sin.

Almost as soon as I was admitted, Gary, a middle-aged business man, befriended me. He had bipolar disorder as well, and he was just recovering from a psychotic episode. He encouraged me and told me to say the Lord's Prayer over and over again when my racing thoughts got worse. He assured me that I would be better soon. He consoled me with the words, "I was much more sick than you are when I admitted myself for help, and look at me now! I'll be leaving in a couple of days!" That was just what I needed to hear.

My medication had been taken from me temporarily, and I was getting worse fast. I tried to say the Lord's Prayer as Gary had suggested, but I couldn't get through it. I would get mixed up and stumble, but I kept trying. I would try to read Bible verses, but it was too hard to concentrate. I certainly wasn't able to memorize, which I tried to do as well. Eventually, I was unable to read at all, and they took my precious Bible away from me.

By this time I had been placed in isolation as I was full-blown psychotic. I thought that I was in a communistic country when they took my Bible away. The inner restlessness made me feel as though I were filled with demons. My whole moral fiber was being ripped apart, and it didn't seem that it could ever be mended again. There were times when I was in isolation, that the evil spirits were so real that I tried to cough or throw up to get rid of them. Then I would scream for Mom to get the door opened, as I needed to wash out my mouth.

Mom and I were locked in this isolation room. Mom wanted to be with me even though she has a problem with claustrophobia. She would be with me from early morning until night.

When I started to get better, I asked some of the nurses if others experienced demons as I had. They told me that everyone, who was as sick as I had been, experienced demons but they didn't know why, of course. I tried to understand it, thinking that maybe the devil was taking advantage of my vulnerability. It seemed so real, but then every hallucination while psychotic was so real to me.

It took longer than average for me to get over my psychosis because I was given haloperidol (Haldol) at first. This was not the great miracle drug for me that it was for others. It became clear to Dr. Jamieson that haloperidol should be replaced by chlorpromazine (Thorazine) which is more sedating. The process of getting over this episode took longer, but it worked.

While psychotic, I was hallucinating all the time. I thought I had had a heart attack and was dying. Across from my isolation room was an examination room complete with examining table and instruments. I thought they were getting the room ready for my open heart surgery. I kept asking Mom to check my pulse as I was sure that I was going to die.

I just couldn't sleep, maybe 10 minutes at a time. Mom would tell me stories that would be nice and soothing. One that I remember was about a farmyard, picket fence, a couple of kids, a cat, dog, cows and the sun shining brightly. I would want her to make the story longer and longer as it was somewhat comforting. She would rub my arms, legs and back in an attempt to help me relax and calm down. This did sometimes put me to sleep, but I would wake up in five or 10 minutes with racing thoughts and hearing voices or else gagging and retching on demons.

Mom bought me some earplugs in the hope that it would help muffle the voices, and I thought that it helped a little.

One day, while in isolation, I was so sick that I didn't even recognize my Mom. I wondered who the stylish lady was. Later, I knew who she was.

Sometimes it seemed to me that the nurses were slow to respond when I thought I needed a drink of water or I would die, or wanted to go to the bathroom. Then I would hyperventilate and panic.

At this time I didn't know what was real and what was not real. I can understand someone committing a crime in that frame of mind. Mom was pinned against the wall by a man who was psychotic. He saw her as an enemy. When a nurse happened in, he let her go. Mom just shrugged it off, but it could have been serious in another setting because he did not know right from wrong at this point.

Most of the time I thought that I was Anti-christ, and this was the last delusion to leave me as I got better. The delusions and hallucinations were absolutely real to me. The end of the world events took place before my eyes. I was horrified by it all.

I thought I was hearing messages from God. When lying on my back, I received messages from God. Then I would turn on my right side and relay the messages. When lying on my left side, I was indifferent. Because of the unpardonable sin which I thought I had committed back in the apartment by placing candles as if to worship Satan, I thought that I was going to be the Anti-christ. I was always wanting to help people, so I would lie on my right side and warn people that they should beware of me because soon I would be the Anti-christ. I'd say, "You have to serve the Lord no matter what happens. Don't be deceived by ME. I'm warning you now, so that when I become the Anti-Christ, you won't be fooled, but will stay true to God!" Then I would turn over to my indifferent side totally exhausted by what had just gone on. I went through this ritual of relaying messages when on my right side then turning to my left side to rest, then on my back to get God's message over and over again.

The sheets represented purity to me, a spiritual quality that I cherished. I would sometimes do gross things such as urinating on the floor. When the nurse would come in and clean up, my delusions made me think that this was an act of worship to the Anti-christ. I felt that right now I was a child of God, but soon I would be the Anti-christ, the most evil person in the world. What a horrible, frightening thought!

The light in my room was on all the time, so I would imagine I was being brainwashed. Other times I would think that the light was for sun-tanning, and I would take off my clothes for sun-tanning. It was all weird! There were NO happy delusions! They were either replusive, degrading, terrifying or evil. I sometimes felt like an animal, a monkey or an alligator. I was totally miserable. No one knows, who has not experienced it, how a person suffers in this condition. Maybe, as you read this, you will be laughing or at least snickering at all my foolish and ridiculous thinking and antics, but it really is a tragic illness. I was no longer in control. I was not me. I was always someone or something else, evil or repulsive.

I could not even give myself a shower or dress myself. I couldn't organize my thoughts. I was terrified when I heard a voice say to me, "Cindy, open the third seal and read it." I didn't have my Bible, and I became very agitated and cried. "I can't remember it. I can't quote it." Then the voice sneered, "If you can't quote that Scripture, you WILL BECOME THE ANTI-CHRIST!!" I would be responsible for everyone turning against God, and I would be condemned to hell forever. The terror I felt can not be described.

Sometimes I would stare out the window, trying not to blink my eyes. I thought they were analyzing my mind and that I was going to be helping to find a cure for mental illness. Another time, I thought that I was a guinea pig being used by scientists for testing new drugs for curing mental illness. I really can't begin to tell all the hallucinations and delusions that I had. They were legion.

By the end of two weeks I was moved back with the others. I hadn't been smoking while psychotic; I seemed to have forgotten about that during all the turmoil. But now I was craving cigarettes again. I wanted so desperately to quit smoking that I'd drive the nurses to distraction. One minute I would tell them not to give me a cigarette. Then when they listened to that and refused to give me a cigarette upon request, I would beg until they would relent. Then I'd refuse to take it, but ask for it in a few minutes. The nurses complained to my doctor about the trouble I was giving them. It was decided that I was not ready for that kind of discipline.

Finally, after five weeks, I was well enough to go outside for walks and rides with my folks. It was spring, and once again the grass was so-o-o beautiful. I kept exclaiming to my folks how beautiful everything was. The beauty of it all was again magnified to an unrealistic degree. I was somewhat hypomanic again.

After six weeks in the hospital, I came home for awhile before going back to Fargo to enter business college once again.

Chapter 23

PICKING UP THE BROKEN PIECES

(Cindy) Wednesday, July 5, 1984

After discharge from hospital, I went home for a few days before going back to Fargo where I re-entered business college for the fourth time. This time I finally managed to complete the course. When I first entered, I planned to take the legal secretarial course. By the time I graduated, I was thankful that I managed to complete the clerk-typist, receptionist course. It was a major victory for me, and it made my family happy. It was not the college degree that I had planned, but it was an accomplishment considering the type of year it had been. I didn't have much self-esteem or self-confidence left, but getting through the course helped a little. I graduated Friday, December 21, 1984. It has been almost four years since that graduation, and I'm still struggling with self-esteem, but each year gets better.

Monday, January 7, 1985

After my graduation, I had to find an office job. I succeeded in doing this, in spite of the fact that 80 other people had applied for this position. This gave my self-confidence a boost, but it was short-lived. I was not ready for such a responsible position. As if this wasn't enough I foolishly took a part-time job at a convenience store in the evenings. My judgment was still in need of improvement. I had gone into a moderate high after I started working, and gradually slid into a moderate low before I was laid off. My boss said that he would give me a recommendation as an outgoing, pleasant receptionist, but he needed an experienced bookkeeper. He gave me the option of staying in sales, but I chose to leave.

It was a much needed job, and now I was without work, except for my part-time night job.

I was taking my medication faithfully, but it took awhile to find an anti-depressant that worked best for me. It has turned out to be wellbutrin. Lithium has kept me stabilized, so I haven't had any manic bouts since losing my office job.

Eventually, I got a job as a clerk in a hardware store. At the same same I did telemarketing in the evenings. Then, weekends, I started doing respite care of mentally handicapped people. These three jobs kept me going until January of 1987.

Monday, January 5, 1987

My new full-time position was that of receptionist for an insurance company which I had for three and a half years. At first I was having trouble remembering names and sometimes even the messages of those who called. This was serious! When I asked Dr. Jamieson about it, he told me that sometimes the medication can cause this. Fortunately, I was able to take a smaller dosage, which helped alleviate the problem.

Each year I find that I am able to cope with situations better, am more comfortable with people and experience times of happiness more often than the previous year. Feeling happy is the first step on the escalator to the dizzy heights of the manic merry-go-round, so I still get a little concerned if I wake up and feel like getting up and looking forward to the day.

I am terrified of the manic side of the illness. The first feeling soon becomes the life-threatening nightmare that I have described. However, my life is becoming more enjoyable for which I thank God.

It has taken about five years for me to get stabilized on medicine. The combination of lithium 750mg, tegratol 600mg and wellbutrin 300mg is perfect for me. Perhaps the reason it has taken so long to get me on the right combination and dosage is that it took so long for my illness to be diagnosed. For others, it may take only 30 days, months, or a year.

It has been learned that medicine will help alcoholics whose alcoholism stems from mental illness. I have a friend who was diagnosed as just being an alcoholic who is now stabilized and well on the same combination of medicine that I am taking (lithium, tegratol and wellbutrin). Alcoholism is often a symptom of mental illness. Other abuses is often a symptom of mental illness. Other abuses, such as child abuse, family abuse, and drug abuse sometimes, if not always, stem from mental illness which **can be treated!**

During the summers and weekends when Mom was with me, she would drag me out of bed on Sunday morning so we could go to church. I would be upset when Mom would sign those little cards with my name, address and telephone number. We were looking for a friendly church. When I was at St. Luke's, and was allowed to leave the hospital for periods of time, we would walk to the church across the street. This pastor visited me once in the hospital, and gave me $20 and a marker for my Bible. That meant so much to me!

A pastor from another church visited or attempted to visit me at my apartment and also at the hospital. I am now attending this church. I am given the opportunity of playing the piano for Sunday services. This gives me a feeling of belonging and worth.

For a couple years as I was getting better, I had such a compassion for people who, I thought, were poor and less fortunate. I would help them as much as I could. I was lonely too, and I looked on these kids as my friends.

Although I was trying to help others and wasn't doing anything wrong, I realize now that it gave others in the apartment building the wrong impression of the kind of girl I was — not that they cared. Sometmes when I would come home from work, five or six young people would be sitting on the steps waiting for me. A battery had been stolen from a car, and my landlord blamed these young people. He told them to stay away, or he would call the police. They didn't come back after that.

It is still hard for me to accept that I have a mental illness. There is such a stigma connected to the words, MENTALLY ILL! I would like to make a difference in this world by helping to educate people about mental illness. I would certainly like my illness to be better understood. I pray that there will be more money for research for new and better medicine which will work for everyone suffering from all types of mental illness.

I have learned that mental illness remains the most under-funded major illness in America, in terms of treatment and research. So much needs to be learned. There is a need for understanding and compassion, not ridicule and indifference. Much is being learned about brain chemistry by the scientists. Hopefully, there will be a breakthrough for the other major mental illness, schizophrenia. From my experience, I feel there is nothing worse than not being able to control one's thoughts and actions. The essence of my being was gone.

Statistics report that nearly one in five people suffer from some form of mental illness requiring professional treatment. I personally feel that this must be a conservative estimate. People who have this illness do not seek the help of doctors. I had the classic symptoms of manic-depressive illness which my mom described in detail. Even so, the doctor did not diagnose my illness. After I was seen in both moods, the diagnosis was made. How often does this happen? Fear of the stigma attached to mental illness is a major reason why many people refuse to seek help. I certainly didn't want to go to a psychiatrist. A very large segment of our society is suffering silently, unable to speak for themselves.

Education is needed to let people know that the major mental illnesses such as bipolar disorder and schizophrenia are caused by biochemical disorder in the brain. The cause is biological, not psychological in origin. This information should, hopefully, help stimulate concern, interest and money needed for research. I wish there were more doctors like Dr. Jamieson who has been doing so much to educate people as well as treat the illness.

The attitude of people towards those with mental illness and toward the illness itself needs changing. I've learned the hard way. It would have helped so much if people could have understood and reached out to me and my family in understanding and compassion. It is my desire to help make people aware of this illness through this book, and whatever other way that God may want to use me. My mother and I are now speaking in churches, Christian Women's Clubs and other organizations.

My family has been through so much with me these last years. I have the greatest parents and brothers in the world! I knew I could depend on them even when I thought that I didn't want anything to do with them. My folks never gave up on me. My mom spent her summers and weekends with me even though my antics and hostility were such that only a mother like mine could put up with it. She always tried to encourage me to look on the bright side when there appeared to be no bright side, and she was always there for me whenever I needed her — which was most of the time!

Chapter 24

A MOTHER'S PERSPECTIVE

Saturday, May 12, 1984

When I was in high school, there was a picture in one of my textbooks of a mentally ill girl with scraggly hair standing with her nose pressed against the wall, with the caption MENTALLY ILL. This picture of dejection was indelibly etched in my mind as, down through the years, whenever I heard about mental illness, that picture came to mind. This picture came to life! While I was in the isolation room with Cindy in her psychotic state, she would walk up to the wall, and stand with her nose almost touching it. I could not stand to see that! I tried to get her to sit by me, but she would pull away, and go back to that same position. Of all the things she did while psychotic, this was the most heart-wrenching for me. When she got better, I asked her why she did that? What was going on in her mind? She didn't know. She remembered why she did other things, but couldn't tell me why she did that.

I didn't want Cindy to go through those horrible experiences alone, so I was given permission to be with her. She had so many fears, the worst being fear of evil spirits. There were times when she appeared to be demon possessed when retching and gagging on demons. Cindy was and is a committed Christian. It was not demon possession, but rather mental illness due to biochemical brain disorder.

The strongest and most persistent delusion that she had was the belief that she would be the **Anti-Christ**. As she got better, she would ask, "I'm not the **Anti-Christ**, am I? That's ridiculous, isn't it?" I assured her that what she was experiencing was just part of her illness.

When she was allowed back into the dayroom with other patients, she had trouble following conversaton. She could not watch television as it was confusing and frustrating. Soft music, and later playing the piano herself, was good therapy. Piano had been such an important part of her life, so it was wonderful to hear her play again.

Cindy was able to leave the hospital June 24, six weeks after entering. She came home for a week or so, and then went back to Fargo to continue business college.

One pastor asked Oscar and me if we were ashamed of our daughter's illness? I was a little resentful of the question and replied that I was not in the least ashamed. Why should we be? Just because people lack knowledge? Why should a disorder of the brain be any different from a disorder of the pancreas, the heart or any other part of the body?

The person suffering from a brain disorder can no more help the symptoms of confusion and abnormal or bizarre behavior than a person suffering from a heart attack can help the symptoms of pain, shortness of breath and panic he experiences. We need more education about mental illness.

Dr. Nancy Andreason, author of the book, *The Broken Brain*, states, "The brain is the source of everything that makes us human, humane, and unique. It is the source of our ability to speak, to write, to think, to create, to love, to laugh, to despair, and to hate." In other words, the mind *makes* the person!!

Sometimes the brain malfunctions. Do we need to be ashamed of that? The production of chemicals (neurotransmitters and neurohormones) is one of the many functions of the brain. Some of these chemicals control the moods. Sometimes this biochemical factory malfunctions making a chemical imbalance producing schizophrenia, bipolar disorder and some other mental illnesses. It has happened to over 40 million people. Why should there be a stigma against those who have this illness? It is not caused by weakness, lack of morality, lack of will power, or some traumatic happening, or overindulgent or neglectful parents. The cause is physical, not psychological. Yet people are so embarrassed for those suffering with the illness that they have trouble facing them, or their families. I just read a book written by a pastor who has a schizophrenic son. In 1977, when it was written, the psychiatrist blamed the father for his son's illness. In 1981, John Hinckley's parents were blamed by the psychiatrist for their son's behavior. He told the Hinckley's to bar their son from coming home because he needed to stand on his own two feet. His parents were too overindulgent. You know the result of that! Mentally ill people *need* their family's help.

Tough love does not work for the mentally ill! They are **unable** to shape up or take control of their lives. We parents need to understand that. Punishment does not work. We would not threaten someone who had cancer. It is just as unreasonable and cruel for the mentally ill.

We are so thankful for Cindy's psychiatrist who is part of the third revolution in psychiatry, the new science of chemical treatment. It works! The myths and misinformation handed down from generation to generation make mental illness the most misunderstood of disabilities.

I am so grateful for the hope patients afflicted with bipolar disorder have because of the research that is being done in the field of biopsychiatry. Lithium is a successful treatment in most cases. I was beginning to wonder if it would work for Cindy as it was taking so long, but it did. Psychotherapy doesn't help bipolar illness. Medicine, not talk, is needed.

No one knows, unless they have gone through it, the heartache and suffering we went through seeing our precious daughter going through this kind of torture.

When we lost our businesses, there was a stigma connected to that, causing people to pull away. Then Cindy's illness, coming on the heels of that, widened the rift. Stigma against people who are mentally ill is as Shakespeare put it, "The unkindest cut of all!"

While all our troubles were piling up, it is difficult to find words to express how alone I felt. The picture that has come to mind to depict this loneliness is one of happy people driving and walking along a road talking, laughing, smiling and enjoying life; while my family and I were lying in the ditch, seemingly abandoned, hurting beyond words from the blows of life, and there was no one who stopped to help us. This sounds melodramatic, but that's how I felt. I don't really know how I would have treated someone else in a similar situation, so I must not be too judgmental. I'm sure, however, that the experience has made me much more sensitive to the pain others go through.

My two sisters were lifesavers to me. Emy called everyday long distance during that terrible year. I could pour my heart out to her, and she would know the right thing to say. She let me know about people with bipolar illness who were living normal lives because of lithium treatment. She had the people in her church praying for Cindy. I received calls and letters from some of them assuring me that they were praying faithfully for Cindy. Emy's sympathetic ear and the encouragement she was able to give, helped me through each day. Irene's prayers and calls of encouragement meant so much to me. One day she called to tell me that when she had prayed for Cindy that day, a calm and peace came over her, making her believe that Cindy would be well. The call came at one of the worst times when Cindy was gone, so it was just what I needed to hear. There were times when I, too, would have an unexplained peace in the midst of the worst times. The only comfort I had was knowledge that people were praying.

Shortly after Cindy came back from New York, I received a call from a lady who asked if Cindy had become a prostitute while in New York. I assured her, as emphatically as I could without being nasty, that she most certainly had **not**! She had seen Cindy, and she told me that Cindy didn't seem herself. She wondered if religion and her crusade against the book in high school caused her illness. I explained that her illness was caused by a chemical imbalance. I told her that the brain releases chemicals and uses them to keep our bodies and minds in good working condition. If there is a chemical imbalance, bipolar illness or some other mental disorder may result. Then she wondered if there was mental illness in our family? I explained that a person can have a tendency or predisposition to the illness, the same as diabetes, heart disease, cancer and many other diseases. I believe this lady expressed the views of the people in general. Although I'm not sure she cared, I told her that there is medicine for successful treatment. It has been learned that no amount of talking, psychotherapy, or counseling will help the illness itself — only medication such as lithium. It's strange that with any other illness a person is surrounded with love and concern. With mental illness there is silence. You find yourself alone in your grief. No one is immune from this illness.

At one point Cindy asked me, "How could I have gotten such a horrible illness? I would rather have cancer or anything else!" I told her that she had inherited a gene that made her susceptible to the illness, and God allowed it to happen even though he could certainly have changed that gene. He has rather promised to be with us and to help us day by day through the trials. Ordinarily, I think He allows life to go on in its natural order.

One of Cindy's expressions during these last years while she was sick was, "The day I die is the day I'll be happy!" It began to sound like a recording. However, while she was in isolation at the hospital, it changed to a more desperate, "Mom, I really WOULD like to go to be with Jesus. This life is unbearable!"

Uncontrolled, this illness is worse than death! Cindy was pulled down to the depths of despair for months; then jerked up, sometimes overnight, to the heights of frenzied activity, in both phases rendered incapable of coping with the everyday-experiences of life. I am so glad that she was born at a time when help was available. Fifteen or 20 years ago there was little or no hope for people with this illness.

There will be new and better medication than lithium in years to come, Cindy's doctor says.

There is a new medicine called anafranil which is now used to treat people with obsessive-compulsive disorder. It is successful in 90 percent of the cases. I trust that the stigma which is so cruelly associated to mental illness, will be part of the dark past. Because of lithium, Cindy and more than 40 million like her will be able to live normal lives.

There appears to be a great need to educate the general public about mental illness. Pastors, educators, police, attorneys and legislators seem to require more information.

The silence about mental illness isolates not only individuals, but entire families. There is a need to know that even those who suffer from the most serious mental illnesses — schizophrenia, manic depression and severe depression — can regain normal lives, hold jobs, have families and be active members of their communities. Some very well known names of creative people afflicted with manic-depression are Abraham Lincoln, Winston Churchill, Vivian Leigh, Ernest Hemingway, Patty Duke, and Connie Francis, to mention a few.

It has not been easy for Cindy and me to put down on paper what went on during these dark, unhappy years. Time has not yet healed all the wounds. Also, it is difficult to bare one's soul so openly about the heartbreak and pain.

I hope and pray that this journal will help to educate and give encouragement to others suffering with this illness. It is our hope that people will be able to more readily recognize the symptoms and get help much sooner than Cindy did. It is also our prayer that people will have a better understanding of the illness, so that it will be easier to reach out in warmth and compassion to those afflicted with this dreadful disease.

Chapter 25

A MOTHER'S PRAYER

Dear God, I can understand your bringing us to our knees
By the pain of losing our material things.
I can understand the need for being humbled
By taking away the encumbrances that can hinder us from keeping
Our eyes fixed on You, and the things that are of eternal value.
I can understand the love of the One who knows the end from the beginning;
The One whose "eyes run to and fro throughout the whole earth
To show Himself strong in behalf of those who love Him."

But, God, I am having trouble understanding why our daughter,
Who wanted to live a life that would be pleasing to You,
Who wanted to use the talent You gave her to glorify Your Name,
Who wanted to attend a Christian college to prepare for Your service,
Would be afflicted with such a hideous illness?

An illness that robbed Your child and ours of the ability to have the love, joy, peace, patience, goodness and mercy that You promised.
An illness that reversed each attribute to something evil: hate, unhappiness, unrest, impatience, degradation, misery and numbness.

God, she is appalled and heartbroken by all that she said and did
While she was unable to control her thoughts and actions!

And there is nothing that can change that.
But, God, I know that You can wipe away the tears and wash away the dreadful memories.

Please, dear God, help me to understand and "to see Your goodness in the Land of the Living."
Make something good come from all the sorrow and suffering that Cindy
And all of her loved ones have been through these years.

I love You, and I do trust Your promise that "all things work together for good to them that love God."
Hear my humble prayer in Your time,
And give me the strength to wait patiently and in anticipation.
In Thy Name, I Pray. Amen.

Chapter 26

EPILOGUE

October, 1990

Through it all, God was close by, watching in loving concern, carrying us when physically exhausted, comforting us when emotionally drained and supplying all our needs.

When pacing the floor, wringing my hands and crying to God for help, He would give comfort through verses that would come to mind such as, "Thou wilt keep him in perfect PEACE whose mind is stayed on Thee." One day I found myself repeating the words of Silas Marner, "If'n I'd only trusten! If'n I'd only trusten!" I taught this classic novel years ago and in my time of trouble the story and events of Silas's life that prompted him to groan, "If'n I'd only trusten!" surfaced to remind me that if we trust God, He will work all things for good. Excerpts from sermons, long forgotten, would pop into my head containing some lesson or words of encouragement that I needed right then.

David wrote in the Psalms, "I had fainted had I not believed to see the goodness of the Lord in the LAND OF THE LIVING. Wait on the Lord; be of good courage, and He will strengthen thine heart; wait, I say, on the Lord." Those words of confidence gave comfort. And now we have seen the goodness of the Lord in the land of the living. Cindy is well, stabilized on medicine, speaking at churches and Christian Women's clubs, working full time and using her talent as pianist in the church that she attends. Her brothers are self-employed. Her dad is in the process of building a car wash, and I am still director of a DAC for mentally retarded adults. God is worthy of our trust.

By the way, Cindy got her car back from New York, but not her kitty. Pastor Ken Brown who had a ministry in New

York was coming to our neighboring town to help move his son and family back to New York. When asked, he graciously agreed to bring Cindy's car home, though I'm sure he had reservations considering all the miles the car had traveled with little upkeep. Even so, he and the car made it without incident.

God is good and worthy to be praised!

Chapter 27

BIPOLAR AFFECTIVE DISORDER

Dr. John Jamieson

This chapter has been written, at the request of Cindy and her mother, in the hope that the reader has been stimulated to learn more about this fascinating mental disorder which has wreaked havoc in the lives of so many.

Bipolar affective disorder is the new name for the mental illness formerly known as manic-depressive illness. The new name is more correct as the older term included patients who suffered from attacks (episodes) of depressive illness only. Patients who have never had elevated moods (manic or hypomanic episodes) and who suffer from depressive episodes only, are now said to be suffering from unipolar affective disorder. It appears likely that the two conditions are separate disorders, but they may be mere variants of the same disorder.

Abnormal Moods v. Normal Moods

Everybody becomes depressed sometimes and this is not abnormal. If you suffer a bereavement, if you lose a good friend, if you fail an important examination, if you are fired from your job or if your marriage breaks up, you are likely to feel very unhappy. It is common for this kind of unhappiness to be referred to as depression, but this type of depression is not an illness. It does not usually require psychiatric care. Under these circumstances you may benefit from counseling by a psychiatrist, psychologist, clergyman or friend, but you are not mentally ill. Time alone is the great healer for this type of normal depression

Similarly, everybody gets elated, joyful or happy at times. These elevations of mood will be produced by the arrival of good friends, the birth of a son or daughter, successes of various kinds or the acquisition of property, wealth etc. These pleasant, elated and sometimes almost giddy states, are quite normal and are natural responses to good fortune and success. You are not necessarily mentally ill because you feel wonderfully happy at these times.

How then do we differentiate normal mood fluctuations from moods indicative of mental illness? Fortunately differentiation is usually easy although, in some cases, it can be very difficult. Normal mood changes are usually clearly related to significant life events and are relatively brief in duration. For example the arrival of a new baby will usually cause the parents great happiness for a few days, but the elation will usually subside to a more normal level as they become absorbed again in the day to day business of earning a living and caring for the baby.

If an individual appears to be in a state of great happiness or unhappiness for more than a few days, and if there appears to be no obvious reason for the persistent and marked change in mood, one might reasonably begin to suspect that illness is the cause. However, the illness causing the mood change may not be a mental illness. Many physical illnesses, such as thyroid disorder, can produce prolonged changes in mood and patients should be seen by a physician to exclude as far as possible those conditions which may mimic mental disorder.

Some Psychiatric Terms

At this point it is necessary to introduce some psychiatric terminology. Learning new terms is tiresome, but understanding a few will help in avoiding confusion and irritation. I will use the standard terminology from the Diagnostic and Statistical Manual (DSM). Published by the American Psychiatric Association, the DSM is a rather large volume containing concise descriptions of mental disorders. It is revised and updated about every five years. The most recent edition is referred to as the DSM-III-R (Diagnostic and Statistical Manual, Third Edition, Revised). Using the descriptions of mental disorders and lists of criteria in the DSM-II-R, psychiatrists and other mental health workers are aided in making diagnostic decisions.

Sometimes you may hear a mental health worker talk about an affective disorder or an affective illness. Do not be mystified by the word affective. An affective disorder simply means a mood disorder.

Dividing mental disorders into thinking disorders and mood disorders is one of the most simple classifications. Thinking disorders are sometimes termed cognitive disorders. Of course this is a gross over-simplification as most mental disorders display both thinking and mood abnormalities. However, one type of change is usually more prominent or basic. The reader will have noted that, although Cindy was at times suffering from disordered thinking, the basic disorder was one of mood.

When a patient's thinking is divorced from reality, he or she is said to be psychotic (i.e. suffering from psychosis). The DSM-III-R states that the term psychotic refers to a mental state in which there is "Gross impairment in reality testing and the creation of a new reality." It is well known that a cough is a symptom of many respiratory illnesses but we do not refer to a cough itself as an illness. Similarly, it should be clearly understood that psychosis is only a symptom of mental illness and is not to be thought of as an illness itself. The word "crazy" is the layman's term for psychotic, but crazy is too loosely used in ordinary parlance. For instance one might refer to a friend as a "crazy guy" without implying that the friend is mentally ill.

Cindy was clearly psychotic during her last hospitalization in St. Luke's Hospital, Fargo in May of 1984. Cindy and her mother give an extremely good description of her horrendous and frightening disturbance of thinking. Her psychotic symptoms were of two main kinds — delusions and hallucinations. Cindy heard voices which, although not real to others, were nevertheless very real to her. When the senses play such tricks, we refer to these unreal sensations as hallucinations. In Cindy's case the hearing senses were playing tricks on her — she was therefore suffering from auditory (hearing) hallucinations. The auditory hallucinations were so severe and seemed so real that she tried using earplugs in the hope that the voices would be muffled. It is not surprising that she found the plugs of little help as the voices were coming from (i.e. originating in) her brain and not her ears. Cindy also suffered terribly from bizarre and baseless beliefs. These false beliefs are termed delusions. The DSM-III-R defines a delusion as, "A false personal belief based on incorrect inference about external reality and firmly sustained in spite of what almost everyone else believes and in spite of what constitutes incontrovertible and obvious proof or evidence to the contrary." For example, during more of the last hospitalization, Cindy believed she was "the Anti-christ." She had many, many more delusions — as she said, "they were legion."

Episodes of Mood Disorder

A relatively prolonged fluctuation of mood in a patient with bipolar disorder or other mood disorder is termed a mood episode. Prolonged and unwarranted elevations of mood are termed episodes of mania. If the elevations of mood are mild but nevertheless inappropriate and prolonged, they are termed hypomanic episodes. Some patients with bipolar disorder have manic and depressive episodes, some have hypomanic and depressive episodes and some have only manic episodes. It is important to note that the diagnosis of bipolar disorder is made only when the patient has had manic or hypomanic episodes. Patients who have had only depressive episodes are said to have unipolar depression (sometimes called major depression). Some patients will have only depressive episodes to begin with and will therefore be thought to have unipolar depression. If these patients later develop a manic or hypomanic episode, the diagnosis is then changed to one of bipolar disorder. Presently there is no reliable method of predicting which unipolar depressives will eventually turn out to be bipolar. This explains Cindy's first psychiatrist's difficulty at the initial consultation on the 28th of January, 1983. At that point in time, Cindy was in an episode of depression and the psychiatrist was unable to get any convincing history of periods of elevated mood (hypomania or mania). Although he settled for a diagnosis of depressive disorder (unipolar depression), he clearly stated in his chart notes that bipolar disorder was a possibility. Wisely, he did not alarm Cindy or her mother with his suspicion and certainly, considering the inadequate evidence of bipolar disorder at that time, the prescription of lithium would not have been justified. Moreover, it seems obvious from Cindy's account of her feelings that she would have dismissed even a tentative diagnosis of bipolar disorder and would have refused a trial of lithium. At that first consultation, therefore, an antidepressant (desipramine) was prescribed. On Cindy's third visit (February 22, 1983) her psychiatrist was still unable to make the definitive diagnosis but entered the following note in the chart, "Monitor for possible Bipolar Disorder." Cindy failed to keep her appointment four weeks later and discontinued the antidepressant. The depressive episode persisted until the 27th of May, when she suddenly switched into hypomania. She did not see her psychiatrist again until June 21, 1983, by which time her hypomania was marked by belligerence towards her psychiatrist. The proper diagnosis was then made and appropriate treatment (lithium) was prescribed but, unfortunately, Cindy was not able to accept the advice.

Depressive Episodes

The symptoms (what the patient feels) and signs (what others observe) of depressive episodes vary from patient to patient but individual patients tend to show the same collection (constellation) of symptoms and signs during each episode. For example a patient showing a certain kind of delusion during a depressive episode will tend to display delusions with similar content during subsequent episodes of depression.

During depressive episodes patients usually suffer from depressed mood but, oddly enough, some do not complain of depressed mood. It is possible that those who do not complain of depression are not aware of their depressed mood, while others may be unwilling to admit to being depressed. Some patients fail to recognize or admit to depression because in the past they have only experienced brief periods of depressed mood in response to unhappy situations. They protest saying, "How can I be depressed when I have nothing to be depressed about?" These patients will tend to focus on the physical symptoms of depression which include fatigue, sleep disturbance, constipation, indigestion, headache, various aches and pains and loss of appetite or excessive eating.

A general slowing of mental and physical activity, called psychomotor retardation, is commonly seen during depressive episodes in bipolar patients. A few patients, will have no significant psychomotor retardation but instead will show considerable mental and physical agitation. In Chapter 19, Cindy gives a good account of psychomotor retardation. "I could hardly get out of bed. Taking a shower, dressing, combing my hair became an almost impossible task. It was hard for me to lift my arm to comb my hair," she wrote.

Depressed patients often have disturbances of the sleep pattern. This can take the form of insomnia but also can consist of excessive sleeping (hypersomnia). In the preface and in the first chapter, Cindy's mother describes the hypersomnia which was one of the first features of Cindy's illness. It became so severe in high school that her parents eventually took her to the Mayo Clinic for another opinion.

Depressed patients often display markedly diminished interest or pleasure in all, or almost all, activities. This is generally referred to as apathy and will sometimes be present in the absence of any specific complaint of depressed mood. Gross incapacity to experience pleasure is called anhedonia.

Manic and Hypomanic Episodes

The signs and symptoms of a manic episode are much more dramatic. The mood is elevated and expansive. Most patients with mania (usually referred to as manics — not maniacs) are very active physically. They have boundless energy and require little or no sleep. Although manics sleep only a few hours each night they do not complain of insomnia — on the contrary they are usually very proud of the fact that they need so little sleep. The patient is excessively fond of meeting, talking and generally communicating with others. Cindy describes how, in the streets of New York, she accosted strangers, asking their names, addresses and telephone numbers and "sometimes made arrangements to meet them in the park!" In chapter five, Cindy says that after finding her money she rushed to Blimpey's and "told everybody everything." The same need to communicate will often lead to numerous and lengthy telephone calls to casual acquaintances at very inappropriate hours! The resulting telephone bills can be astronomical! Judgment is impaired early in the episode and leads to excessive spending, bad investments, reckless driving, sexual indiscretions, inability to keep promises, magnanimity, grandiosity and generally irresponsible and unwise behavior. The patient has a rosy, overly optimistic view of the world and unrealistic expectations about the future. Feelings of omnipotence and omniscience are common. In milder manic states (hypomanic states) the patient may be quite creative and successful. Such patients are full of ideas and schemes and are frequently quite engaging in conversation. They lack the usual social inhibitions and will readily approach strangers on any pretext. It is clear that Cindy behaved in this way in the streets of New York and as a result fell into the company of many unsavory and dangerous characters. Hypomania is usually a pleasurable and almost addictive state.

In chapter 19, Cindy writes: "I started going to the parks to sit and look at the grass, trees and little animals scampering about. Everything looked so fresh and beautiful. I was entranced by the beauty of the shimmering leaves in the sun. I felt so in tune with nature. It was an exhilarating and delicious feeling. It made me forget the horrible winter I had just gone through."

Depressed patients are almost always aware of being ill or that something is amiss. By contrast, manic and hypomanic patients are usually unaware of their illness. This lack of awareness is usually referred to as loss of insight and is evident early in manic and hypomanic episodes. Loss of insight creates great difficulties in managing these patients It is extremely difficult to get them to agree to hospitalization and attempts to treat them on an out-patient basis are frequently futile and frustrating. In most states it is nearly impossible to get a court order to hospitalize a patient who is only hypomanic. This was the case with Cindy in mid-July of 1983. The doctor who testified at her mental health hearing clearly knew that the court had no power to hospitalize her when she was only hypomanic.

Cindy writes: "At my next hearing, the doctor did as he promised. He testified in my favor. I did not have to be locked up. The judge told me that I was court ordered to take lithum. I promised to take my lithium faithfully. With that hollow promise I was free to go." Needless to say, Cindy's hypomanic state of mind made her unable to keep her promise!

Unlike hypomanic patients, manic patients present less of a management problem, as while in court and in the presence of the judge, they will usually conduct themselves in such a fashion as to leave the court in little doubt about the danger of their not being committed! Manic patients (and some hypomanic patients) can seldom accept the advice of their defending attorney. They tend to ignore their attorney's advice to remain silent and will frequently and improperly interrupt the proceedings with noisy, threatening language thereby revealing severely impaired judgment and a potential for dangerous behavior. They usually insist on getting into the witness box where the state's attorney can easily expose the bizarre features of their illness.

There is no clear dividing line between hypomanic and manic states. In hypomania the mood disturbance is not sufficiently severe to cause marked impairment in social or occuptional functioning and there are no delusions. The hypomanic patient can be thought of as suffering from mild mania.

The Natural Course of Bipolar Disorder

The term 'natural course' of any illness refers to the course the illness would take if left untreated. Some illnesses such as the common cold get better spontaneously while others such as meningitis and cancer, frequently end in death. By now the reader should understand that the natural (i.e. untreated) course of bipolar disorder consists of episodes of mania (or hypomania) and perhaps episodes of depression. In untreated cases these episodes (manic, hypomanic or depressive) usually last for several months. Switches from mania to depression and vice versa can be gradual but can also occur within a few hours. Cindy experienced at least one such sudden switch of mood on May 27, 1983. She writes: "Two weeks before spring break, one of the girls at school and I started talking and made plans to attend a show that evening. As I was getting ready to go, I suddenly felt so exceptionally happy and felt so good about myself. Everything seemed so wonderful, even glorious. I believed it was that I had a friend at last. I continued to feel exhilarated, like a new person!"

Between episodes there are often periods of freedom from the illness. These periods of well-being or normalcy are called remissions and may last for weeks to years. Failure to remember that the illness can remit spontaneously has led to many misunderstandings and even tragedies. For example, a patient may, for one reason or another, discontinue medication and be delighted to find that nothing untoward follows.

The patient may then conclude that medication is, or has been, unnecessary and that a cure has been effected when really all that has happened is that the patient has been lucky enough to discontinue medication during a period of remission! The remission may last for years but more often there will be a disastrous recurrence of the illness within a few months.

What Causes Bipolar Disorder?

By now the reader should have a rough idea of the shape and characteristics of this illness and will be asking, "Well, what causes this illness?" Unfortunately the short answer is that we really do not know. There have been many speculations about the cause, but there is no convincing proof that any one set of circumstances produces the illness. However, there is now general agreement among psychiatrists that it is unlikely to be caused by psychological or social problems. There is clear evidence that the illness is familial and that there is a genetic component at work. More research along these lines is urgently required.

It is very probably that bipolar disorder represents a group of conditions rather than one illness with one case. Bipolar disorder will probably turn out to be a group of disorders which look alike but are really different illnesses. Moreover, each one of these disorders may have multiple causes!

Treatment of Bipolar Disease

Difficult as it may be for the professional to deal with the manic or hypomanic patient, it is as nothing when compared to the difficulties faced by relatives. Cindy's mother describes the nightmare well. Relatives feel frantic, powerless, frustrated, betrayed, rejected, abandoned, abused and, although the patient is still alive, they often feel bereaved. It is hard for those with no previous knowledge of the illness to understand what understand what in the world has happened to the patient. There is obvious relief when it is explained to them that the patient is ill and not wicked, irresponsible, sinful or demon-possessed! It is of great help to explain, in no uncertain terms, that bipolar disorder is an illness now believed to be due to a biochemical disorder in the mood-regulating system of the brain and that it is just as genuinely medical in nature as is diabetes mellitus, asthma, or any other medical illness.

Hospitalization is essential for the manic patient in order to protect the patient from himself and others and sometimes to protect others from the patient. Hypomanic patients can occasionally be treated outside the hospital but usually this is only possible when there is already a trusting and well-established relationship with the treating physician. The hospital milieu tends to help patients get some control of themselves. Sometimes it is helpful to restrict visitors as the stimulation by others tends to excite the patient. Cindy seems to have been aware of this as she wrote: "It seemed I would not be as manic or high at night because I would sometimes feel so alone."

For many years the search for effective treatments for bipolar disorder was hampered by the belief that almost all major mental illness was due to psychological or developmental problems. The vast majority of mental health professionals no longer accept this premise and much of this acceptance springs from the obvious though limited success of various medications in controlling these illness.

The one most useful medication for controlling bipolar disorder is lithium. This is marketed in the form of lithium carbonate and, as chemical substances go, it is as simple as chalk (calcium carbonate). It is important to clearly understand that lithium is not addicting in any way. No patient craves lithium and no street drug pusher sells lithium! There is never any difficultly in getting patients to stop taking lithium! On the contrary, the difficulty is in getting them to take lithium and take it consistently. Lithium unfortunately has side effects which are sometimes troublesome and at times even intolerable. Taken in excessive doses and without adequate medical supervision it can be poisonous — but so can table salt! It is essential to monitor the concentration of lithium in the blood during treatment and this, of course, means taking periodic blood samples. Other medications are used in the treatment of the illness or in certain phases of the illness but none are as useful as lithium. A substantial number of patients respond to lithium very well indeed and their lives are transformed. An equally large number seem to get partial benefit and unfortunately some patients show no response whatever to lithium treatment. This variability in response has given rise to some of the speculation that we are dealing with a group of different but look-alike disorders rather than one disorder. I predict that, before the end of the century, lithium will be replaced by much more effective, less troublesome and safer treatments. For the sake of Cindy and all the other Cindy's of the world I pray that this prediction will come true.

Finally a word about psychotherapy. The popular, but outdated, image of the psychiatrist is that of a physician whose main modality of treatment is psychotherapy. Unfortunately formal psychotherapy is of little or no value in bipolar disorder. However, if by psychotherapy one means forming a trusting relationship with the patient and relatives and the exploring of issues surrounding the taking of medication, one has to admit that psychotherapy is extremely helpful though not curative. Being a rather simple-minded physician I prefer not to use the term psychotherapy to describe these interventions which are, after all, only straight forward methods of good patient management and good medical care.